MW00620262

BUTTERFLY RISING

A Journey to Love, Healing, and Freedom from the Cocoon of Codependency

By *GAIL FERGUSON JONES*

Copyright © 2021 URBANE COMMUNICATIONS LLC
All Rights Reserved

ISBN: 978-0-9600613-0-3

Copyright © 2021. Gail Ferguson Jones. All right
reserved.
This book or parts thereof may not be reproduced in any
form, stored in any retrieval system, or transmitted in any
form by any means—electronic, mechanical, photocopy,
recording, or otherwise—without prior written permission
of the publisher, except as provided by United States of
America copyright law.

PRAISE FOR BUTTERFLY RISING

Rising from the ashes of her own experience, Gail Ferguson Jones tells a raw and compelling story of transgenerational suffering that ends in triumph facilitated by truth and fellowship.

Gabor Maté M.D.

Author, "In the Realm of Hungry Ghosts: Close Encounters With Addiction"

Gail Ferguson Jones shares her remarkable journey from the despair of codependency to the triumph of recovery. In these pages is valuable wisdom for anyone who has lost themselves in the addiction struggle of someone they love.

Mastin Kipp,

Functional Life Coach; Author, "Claim Your Power," and "Daily Love. Growing into Grace."

The pain and hopelessness suffered by the loved ones of alcoholics is only made worse when they follow their natural instincts to control the drinking and recovery. No one has more experience in suffering and recovery from relationships with people who abuse alcohol than Gail Ferguson Jones. Gail has transformed her experiences into empathy and understanding that serves as a roadmap to those who find themselves in similar situations. She reaches people not just with her story, but with her love and charisma that made me instantly want to hear more and learn more the first time I had the pleasure of meeting Gail.

Matt Salis,

Author, "soberevolution;" Host, Untoxicated Podcast

In this book, Gail Ferguson Jones describes the suffering she endured by trying to relate to alcoholic family members who had a more powerful relationship with the bottle than with her. The story she has to tell focuses on the traumas that she developed as a result of the abuse and neglect she experienced in these relationships. The best part of the book is where she describes her awakening and how she put an end to her suffering by taking charge of her life. It is an inspiring story of hope, about how people can overcome the intergenerational family patterns of alcoholic families. There is a lot in the book that shows the courage it takes to break out of this codependency trap. I highly recommend this book.

Barry Weinhold,

Psychologist; Author, "Get Real: The Hazard of Living Out of Your False Self."

Gail Ferguson Jones knows the toxic reality of generational addiction and codependency all too well. She's also an inspiring example of someone who has broken the cycle and built a new life of peace, joy and freedom. This book offers a blueprint for those desperate to reclaim their lives from the dysfunction and pain of co-addiction.

Sherry Gaba,

Author, "Love Smacked: How to Stop the Cycle of Relationship Addiction and Codependency;" Former Co-Star of VH1's "Celebrity Rehab with Dr. Drew Pinsky."

To be with Gail's words is like taking a walk with a mindful guide. I have known Gail for a lifetime plus, and her healing truths continue to inspire me to focus within. She is a heroic woman who shares the darkest depths of her soul, but does it with such grace, that we feel safe opening up our own. I highly recommend Butterfly Rising as a healing tool for those seeking insight into a codependent relationship.

Mira Masukawa,

Licensed Marriage and Family Therapist; Author, "Love Grieving: A Healing Workbook for Bereavement."

Gail is such a powerful storyteller whose honesty will crack open your heart to greater compassion and love.

Heather Box,

Co-founder of the Million Person Project; Author, "How Your Story Sets You Free."

Gail has an incredibly potent story living amid the pain and chaos that is family addiction, trauma and codependency. She shares her journey through a lens of such grace, it allows others the beautiful glimpse of hope that awaits them and all of us. Gail's commitment to family recovery is profound and this book should be in the hands of everyone who faces these challenges.

Kate Duffy,

CEO & Founder, Tipping Point Recovery, Inc.

Gail has a spirit of truth wrapped with love that she draws from her experience with addiction and recovery. You will feel her strength in the pages of this book that will inspire you to use your own story to transform your life.

Kimberly Ready,

Co-Founder of Oaks Recovery; Family Trauma Specialist; National Recovery Advocate

Gail's story and her brilliant writing are a healing blessing to the world. When I first met Gail several years ago, she was in a very dark place, anxious and disheartened by her family circumstances.

Over the years that I've prayed with her, guided and mentored her, I've witnessed the miracle of her inner growth and healing. I've been blessed to see her rise from personal despair with beautiful butterfly wings of new awareness and spiritual strength. She deeply transformed her consciousness, from that of victim, to living from a place of wholeness, truth, grace, and love. In this book, Gail shares how this healing transformation is available to anyone. She uses her own recovery as the message she shares with her book, her podcast, and her coaching. h a vessel of love, light, and healing.

The Rev. Dr. Frankie Timmers,

Spiritual Director, Center for Spiritual Living
Morristown, N.J.

DEDICATION

I share these experiences, not in rebuke of those I still love so dearly, but as a gift of forgiveness and redemption for their troubled souls and the earthly pain that drove them to the self-destructive path of addiction.

And as one who has been redeemed by the gift of healing, I have come to know a new freedom. In these pages, I pray that you, too, find the beautiful gift of freedom that is recovery from codependency.

TABLE OF CONTENTS

Part III

Part I

CHAPTER 1

A Hard Fall,
A Wakeup Call

I am the maternal granddaughter of an alcoholic, the daughter of an alcoholic father, and the widow of an alcoholic husband. My grandmother was a stunning beauty. My father was loving and tenderhearted. And I was spoiled when it came to material things by my husband, who was dependable and committed to our family.

All three of these loved ones wanted only to be left to their drinking, without question, challenge, or interruption. Yet, everyone in our family was desperate for them to get sober.

As a child, I wanted to love my grandmother without fear of her drunken mood shifts. My favorite times were spent sitting next to her as she puffed on the cherry tobacco in her pipe, telling me stories of her younger self. But I wanted my grandmother to stop taunting my mother, mocking her only daughter with verbal abuse when she felt my mother stood in the way of her next drink.

I wanted the full adoration of my dad, who I only saw during occasional visits, but without the distraction of his shaking hands as his body shifted its attention to his craving. I loved the tender, daddy-daughter bond we shared when together, but I so wanted him to live free of the shame and sadness that he couldn't hide.

My husband never denied me anything that could be purchased, and he was a doting and devoted father. But my deepest desire, which was for him to be healthy and happy without the crutch of alcohol, was exactly the notion he refused to even consider, despite repeated near-death experiences. It seemed rock bottom was never far enough down for him.

My determination to get him the help he needed was not enough for him to choose sobriety. Even after I finally got him into rehab, he checked out after only two weeks. What I wanted concerning his health didn't matter.

Those of us who have lived with these circumstances can't help but be mystified by the stranglehold substance abuse has on the user's life, thinking, and choices. It's hard to understand why they can't break its grip and why it seems they don't want to.

Alcoholics and drug abusers can't understand the pain their problem causes the rest of us. Instead, they take comfort in their denial while we wallow in fear. There are neurological and physiological hurdles that keep substance abusers continuing on a self-destructive path.

Those of us who suffer the collateral damage of their sickness often think that our troubled parent, spouse, child, relative, or significant other holds the key to our mental and emotional relief. But they don't. We are the gatekeepers to our own peace, health, and happiness. They are the guardians of their own lives.

The longer we try in desperation to shoulder open the door of sobriety for them, the more damage we suffer ourselves. I found this truth out the hard way.

I was shocked beyond belief when the doctor who treated me for more than a decade informed me that I suffered from post-traumatic stress.

"How could that be?" I asked myself, as the appearances of my successful life flashed through my mind. I never served in the military. Never experienced war. Isn't PTSD brought on by the traumas of battle? So, what was she talking about?

But I knew she was right as I thought back on the emotional breakdown that I'd experienced the previous morning. During that moment, I felt a sense of despair I had never known before. I recalled the guttural howl of my own voice while I lay straight-jacketed to my bed by the trauma of recent events.

I recognized how I suffered from the lifelong emotional wounds of shame and blame. The lingering embarrassment of my loved ones' drunkenness. The years of my grandmother blaming my mother, my mother blaming my father, and my husband blaming me for the chaos in our lives.

Until that point, I did not realize the painful burden I carried. The willful denial of the childhood disappointment I thought was behind me. The generational trauma of the years landed on me like a ton of bricks. My soul cried out under its weight. I saw for the first time how blind loyalty and unconditional tolerance threatened my life and could cripple my future.

I had long trusted my doctor with some of the shameful aspects of my family life when seeking referrals for therapeutic counseling. And I took her advice years earlier when she suggested 12-step support. Her counsel was part of the treatment for my earlier diagnosis of high blood pressure, insulin resistance, and excessive weight gain, as I struggled to bring these health challenges under control.

I never imagined how the effects of enabling someone else's destructive habits would have on me. How mentally taxing it was to think I could control their decisions and behavior. How frustrations piled up from making excuses for them. Resentments lingered from giving in to their demands and verbal abuse.

Finally, I had enough. I was pushed to the brink of my ability to cope, and my very life and well-being were on the line. I lived with the constant fear and worry of watching one loved one after another fall into a death spiral that I was helpless to stop. And now, I was no longer willing to sacrifice myself in the name of love.

It was time to get down to the work of recovery. To take a long look inside and find where I lost myself. My self-love. My sense of self-worth. Recognition of my true value. It was time to pursue my own joy and happiness, and it was up to me to reclaim my power. I was determined to be free.

CHAPTER 2

Starting the Climb
From Rock Bottom

The worst day of my life was the most important day of my life.

That morning, I was aroused from my sleep by daylight. I opened my eyes and tried to get out of bed but couldn't.

Suddenly, I heard ear-splitting wails pierce the silence. Then, I realized it was me, crying uncontrollably.

Hours passed as I lay in a sobbing heap in my queen-size, oak, sleigh bed, swaddled in the thick, red and gold comforter that matched the drapes.

Bright and cheerful sunlight poured through the sheer silhouette blinds that decorated the wall-length windows of my bedroom, where I slept alone. I felt the warmth of the daylight beckoning me to rise, but somehow, I couldn't. I felt lost, confused, and helpless, without the desire or willpower to pull me up.

As minutes ticked away, I felt the rays of the sun comforting me, although I couldn't see beyond my tears. The sun beckoned me to rise to its glorious blessedness, but the dreaded news I received the day before, that my husband was checking himself out of rehab early, held me in its grip.

I felt unworthy and undeserving of the sun's life-force.

Eventually, I surrendered to the whispers of the Sun Goddess, who seemed to understand that after so many years of being strong and resilient, my spirit was depleted, and I had no fight left.

A lifetime of love and loyalty had proved fruitless against the demons stalking my family. Now the pain was unbearable.

I realized that if nothing changed, nothing would ever change for me. I knew that I could not change others, but I could make the necessary changes for myself. I could stop expecting from others what I was not willing to do for myself.

Blanketed in the warmth of the morning rays, it dawned on me that this was my rock-bottom moment. It was time for me to rise from the pain and desperation caused by my life of co-addiction.

I committed right then and there that I would make my own life my priority, accepting that I was valuable in my own right, apart from my husband. With this resolve, I wiped away my tears and rose into a new life of healing and freedom from dysfunction.

Just two weeks earlier, I finally got my husband into rehab after more than five years of fruitless interventions, doctor's referrals, and hospital stints in intensive care. Unfortunately, his high-level professional status in the corporate world held him firmly in denial, and his ego insisted that he could handle his problem with alcohol addiction on his own. He believed it.

After my incessant pleas to doctors who treated him during his latest admission to intensive care, they convinced him to get help. I was cautiously optimistic about his chances for survival. After all, how many times does someone have to lie in the hospital with a respirator keeping them alive to recognize his rock bottom? Although he always seemed unfazed by these near-death episodes, despite the strong reactions from his loved ones and family.

I got my husband admitted to a treatment center, halfway across the country, away from everything familiar and all his enablers. This placement allowed him to stay focused on his sobriety and the chance for a healthy future.

However, the day before my sudden meltdown, I got a call from his rehab counselor informing me that my husband was checking himself out of the program before completing the 30 days he'd agreed to. I'll never forget her dire warning: "If he leaves here now, he's going to die." Her prediction eventually proved true. And the next morning, as I faced the reality of the situation, I suffered a visceral reaction to her prognosis.

My doctor later explained to me that my breakdown was caused by my nervous system being in a constant state of fight-or-flight. Following the adrenaline rush of getting my husband through the latest medical emergency, my nervous system crashed, particularly after getting the news that he was refusing the help he needed.

At the same time, my acceptance of that reality ultimately set me free. The news that was so unfortunate for him, was life-affirming for me. And from that day on, I decided to focus on the value of my own life.

If he wasn't willing to fight for his life and appreciate himself as valuable and worthwhile, I realized that I couldn't make that choice for him.

Once I was able to lift myself out of bed and call my doctor for help, I made a commitment to my own health, happiness, and emotional freedom.

I had never heard the word "codependency" before, but as I set out to rediscover myself and live life on my own terms, I learned that I had experienced a lifetime of codependent relationships that were mentally and emotionally dysfunctional and unstable.

I realized that I had never learned to detach from the selfish and self-destructive habits of others. Every generation of my family was conditioned to take responsibility for others at the expense of our own well-being. And we tried to gain control of the alcoholic chaos, which is typical codependent behavior.

As a result, I became comfortable playing the victim role and living in blame and shame. I finally realized, it was time to take my focus and judgments off my loved one and take responsibility for myself. I was a victim only because I chose to be.

Rock bottom is the place where everyone in my same situation reaches their limit of tolerance and enabling. The place of rock bottom is where, as a recovery coach, I hear from family members who are tired of living in fear and resentment and are ready for change.

At the same time, I reached the place of acceptance, understanding the circumstances I could not change. I realized it was my husband's responsibility to save himself. I could not do it for him.

From this turn of events, my goal was to reconnect to my own value and stop covering for my beloved. No more hiding behind my image as the wife of a prominent, worldwide corporate executive. I clearly recognized the hollowness of that window dressing, but I had spent years propping up the impressive image.

My new dreams were not big, but basic, humane, worthy, and true. I desired health, happiness, self-love, and freedom. It's what I deserved, and I was no longer going to deny myself by trying to change my nearest and dearest.

I would no longer live in his pain and trauma, his choice to self-medicate rather than seek help. No longer would I allow what was ailing his spirit to sicken mine. Why had I let his demons chase me too?

I rose from my own rock bottom, and allowed myself to feel my value, to honor my worth, and to live accordingly. What at first seemed like the worst day of my life, turned out to be the best. It was the day I chose the path of recovery.

It was not that I loved my husband less. It was just that I shifted my focus. The compassion that I so lovingly felt for him, I realized I deserved too.

I was no longer willing to accept and excuse verbal and emotional abuse, lies, and gaslighting. No more putting aside my personal ambitions to be available for him. No more hypervigilance as I waited for the next health emergency, while he continued to indulge his life-threatening appetites.

So, while the nature of addiction leaves no room for compassion for others, I learned that I could treat myself with compassion. I did not need to depend on someone else to treat me in the way I deserved. This realization freed me from feeling victimized.

And so, my attention shifted away from the personal problems my husband was unwilling to address, to who I wanted to be as an individual. Healthy and happy.

And the road to discovering my happiness started with self-love. This revelation is where recovery from codependency began for me.

Learning that tough love may be difficult, but it's important to let addicted loved ones suffer the consequences of their actions while giving ourselves the gift of self-love.

If we can't and don't love ourselves, we will always give away our power and live in victimhood.

Self-love and self-worth go hand-in-hand. When we recognize our own personal worth, we no longer use someone else's addiction as an excuse for not living our best life.

Interestingly enough, the key to recovery is the same for both addicts and their loved ones. Awareness. As we become more self-aware, we recognize and accept our value, reclaim our self-esteem, and come to terms with our human imperfections, knowing that we don't have to be perfect to be worthy.

We no longer feel the need to judge others or make comparisons. This understanding opens the door to a grateful heart.

We become thankful for our courage to change, learn, and grow. Grateful for the freedom to let go of controlling anyone else's life or choices. Grateful to surrender to a Higher Power that loves and cares for us unconditionally. And grateful to experience that eternal love in a new way and to be delightfully surprised by how it shows up in our lives.

We finally know that we are valuable and valued. There's no need to rely on others to feel worthy. We can let go of feeling shame, blame, and resentment, no longer living in fear. Loving ourselves and living our value.

But the only way to climb from my codependent rock bottom was to figure out how I got there in the first place.

My recovery started with a walk down memory lane.

CHAPTER 3

Grandma and I Were Robbed

My grandmother was a regal beauty.

Tall and statuesque, with the mocha complexion of her ancestry. Her paternal grandmother was the biracial daughter of a slave owner and was none too pleased with my grandmother's brown-paper-bag coloring, which was too dark for her liking.

By the time of my birth to her only daughter, my 60-year-old grandmother's long silken hair was a wavy, shimmering silver, with the sheen of a calm ocean, rolling down her back.

Her features were fine and her skin flawless. She possessed not only physical allure but a charismatic presence and confident carriage, even after decades of alcoholism. But the stroke she suffered just weeks after my birth left her somewhat debilitated, dragging around her paralyzed left side.

This was the only version of her I knew.

The one who told me bedtime stories of the lynchings she saw from the window of the home her grandmother inherited from her white father. She told these stories as though she was sharing Halloween tales on mischief night. Even though I was barely school age, I somehow recognized that she was deeply wounded by these childhood remembrances. I vaguely understood how the trauma was linked to the drinking that ate at her spirit until it broke her body.

She also lost a baby boy to whooping cough, a common cause of child fatalities in the early Twentieth century. His death led to an early divorce, which was shameful and uncommon at the time. She later remarried and gave birth to my mother, only to find herself widowed soon after, with a toddler to care for.

There's something so special about a grandmother in the eyes of a little one, and from the family history that was relayed to me from a very young age, I felt especially compassionate toward mine. So, while the grandmother I knew was a mean drunk, I felt a special tenderness for her.

Unfortunately, as the saying goes, hurt people hurt people. And hurt her only daughter, my grandmother did. She groomed my mother into codependence, while unwittingly, robbing her of confidence and self-esteem.

Of course, none of us knew the concept, but I can say with certainty now, that I lived with the sad truth of a codependent personality during my upbringing. In hindsight, I can see why my mother seemed guarded and defensive in relationships, even with me, and was extremely judgmental of others. She always seemed pessimistic about life, which led me to believe that my dysfunctional family circumstances were simply my fate.

My mother was always dutiful to the mother whose life she saw slowly slip into loneliness and despair.

My grandmother, the charismatic beauty who was once so smart and admired, burned so many bridges because of her alcoholism that she was abandoned by most every family member and friend.

In my mother's early adulthood, I was told, her emotions were always determined by my grandmother's moods at any given time and place. She learned to always put her mother's wants and needs ahead of her own, and my mother's fear of her mother's anger determined her decision-making.

Under these circumstances, it was no wonder that my mother's view of herself was greatly influenced by her drunken mother's insults and put-downs. She never felt good enough and did not know how to ask for or accept help. And she struggled with the idea of being needed, even by me.

This is the codependent personality that raised me. Was it any surprise that I ended up with an alcoholic father and husband too?

Fortunately, my mother eventually reached her breaking point with my grandmother, but the necessary, though temporary, estrangement from someone so near and dear was heartbreaking. I felt her sad longing for her mother during those times of estrangement when she knew she had to detach.

This pattern repeated itself in my life with my father and my husband.

Codependency requires detachment from the addiction problem of a loved one for the survival of our sanity. We need time and space to learn to make our own needs and wants the priority of our lives.

We must learn turn a deaf ear to the insults and put-downs in order to connect with a sense of worthiness and self-esteem. To get to know and appreciate ourselves as smart, beautiful, and lovable in our own right, and worthy of being treated as such.

There is no reason to allow someone else's moods and attitudes to rob us of our peace of mind and emotional well-being. Unrequited loyalty is never justified. But we are conditioned to believe that love requires such allegiance, even when at our own expense.

My grandmother died in a mental hospital when I was just nine years old, and I missed her for a long time, just because of her standing in my life. She shared with me valuable family history. Unfortunately, she left a sad legacy and hard lessons instead of fond memories.

It's sad that the disease of alcoholism robbed both of us of the most joyful benefits of family relationships. I have no memories of her kissing my skinned knee or giving me valuable advice. She never got to share the wisdom of her life's challenges, or to be a confidant, cheerleader, shoulder to cry on, or cherished friend.

Yes, addiction is a thief. And what it steals from us is so precious that it can never be regained. Such opportunities are lost forever.

But the biggest lesson I learned from my grandmother, codependent mother, father, and husband, is that no one can love me as much as I love myself. It is our own self-love that keeps us from sliding down the slippery slope of addiction or codependency.

Self-love keeps us healthy and strong. It rewards us with loving relationships of our own. Self-love provides the chance to spread love and light instead of hurt and pain. Self-love is its own reward, and no one can take that from us. It is a God-given right. We cannot love others if we don't love ourselves.

I wish my grandmother would have loved herself and had left cherished memories instead of heartache. I wish she could have known what it was like to be an admired and beloved family matriarch.

I wish she had given me a mother who knew what it was like to be happy and whole. A mother who knew how fulfilling relationships could be.

I wish my grandmother knew how much I loved her. My child's eyes recognized the beauty of her soul behind the pain that drove her addiction

CHAPTER 4

Living in Shame and Abuse

I remember the night two NYPD officers came to our Brooklyn apartment and took my mother away, leaving me home alone, not knowing when or if she would return.

My seven-year-old self was scared and confused as I lay in my bed, enveloped in the loneliness of the dark apartment after the police turned off the lights and closed the door behind my mother's exiting back. I was shocked that they would leave me alone to the unknown, but also grateful that I was not taken into child protective services.

Before their arrival, my mother and I were going through our evening ritual. Dinner together at the dining room table, homework completed, and pajamas at the ready.

Our curiosity was piqued when the doorbell rang. Who could it be at that time of night? My mother opened the door leading into the hallway and surveyed the two uniformed officers standing on the other side of the smoked-glass foyer door.

"Yes?" she inquired.

"New York City Police," came the reply. "Are you V.F.?" they asked. She replied in the affirmative. "We need to speak to you."

My mother left our apartment door slightly ajar as she let the officers into the main hallway. All I could hear were voices speaking in even tones, questions, and answers, but there was a tone of measured fear from my mother's side of the conversation. There was uncertainty in her voice.

I didn't know exactly what the topic was, except I was certain it had something to do with my alcoholic grandmother, who my mother packed off to stay with a relative in New Jersey. She stayed with a cousin who was a nurse at a state psychiatric hospital and had no minor children living in her home.

My grandmother had come to live with us several months before. Her drunken escapades got her sent packing by everyone else who initially felt pity for her condition after she suffered a stroke. She had not lived with us since before I was too young to remember, so I was excited to really get to know the woman whose poise and strength in her younger years I had heard so much about.

Being so young, I was at first intrigued by the challenges of her physical condition, but also amazed at her independent spirit and tenacity. That is, until I recognized how she used her circumstances in an alcoholic dance of emotional manipulation.

At first, it was nice to have her home when I arrived from school while my mother worked. I was fascinated as I watched her pack her pipe with cherry wood tobacco. She sat in a rocking chair with me at her knee, as I took in the comfort of the sweet, smoky aroma and her mere presence.

But it was unnerving when my grandmother took me with her on the subway so she could panhandle. She dragged me along as an extreme form of manipulation on her part, the hallmark of an addictive personality.

There was no reason for her to go begging in the streets, dragging her paralyzed limbs, twisted face, and a young child through the subways of New York. As a widow, my grandmother was supported by my grandfather's veteran's pension, and she had no real living expenses while staying with us.

But she played the angles of a poisoned brain, making strangers feel sorry for us as she shook them down for cash.

Meanwhile, I was confronted with the madness of addiction every day that I came home from school. Our elegant apartment was often filled with homeless derelicts off the street. My grandmother invited them in to drink with her after sending them to the liquor store to make her purchases.

Growing up in a city like New York, these were vagrants I was used to avoiding on the street. They were grotesque figures with swollen lips, over-ripened by the years of swilling wine from passed bottles. Their eyes bulged in madness, and to my child's ears, they seemed to speak in gibberish. Their limbs too seemed ready to explode, pumped as they were by the poison trapped inside. Yet their bodies seemed rigged, their organs obviously soaked and drowning in rivers of overconsumption.

Through their flesh, they exuded the toxic odors of fermented grapes and molten yeast. In those days before cigarette smoking was generally taboo, the smell of tobacco on their breath mixed with the strong drink was the cherry atop their unwashed stench.

These sick souls lost anything worth living for in this world and had no bridges left to burn among family and friends after years of self-destructive behavior and social ruin. End-stage disease was written all over them. The clock was running out on their sad existence.

Yet, these were the "friends" my grandmother opened our home and lives to. She felt more privileged because she had a nice home and family to misuse and abuse, which was more than the others could hope for again.

These guests left puke and blood on the toilet and bathroom sink, de-sanitizing every surface they touched with their very being. They stared at me and grabbed at me, all inebriated monsters in my eyes. My fright at the sight of them was their amusement, the life of their party. I was just the innocent foil.

Eventually, my mother questioned the bodily fluids staining the bathroom and my grandmother lied, saying they were hers.

But when I was asked, I broke down in tears. "Grandma had company," I ratted, knowing she had been ordered not to have strangers in the house while my mother was at work, or any other time, for that matter. I felt relieved to fink on my grandmother, who, of course, made friends with our alcoholic next-door neighbors, the superintendents of our apartment building, making the situation even more difficult. I just wanted the nightmare I faced every day after school to end.

Eventually, my second-grade teacher summoned my mother. I had always been a bright and eager student, but she noticed that lately I seemed sullen and distracted. I did not participate with my usual enthusiasm and appeared to be troubled, Mrs. H. told my mother.

In essence, she told my mother that it was obvious there were some problems at home that were making me a nervous wreck. She encouraged my mother to address the situation in a way that was best for me.

At the same time, family acquaintances spotted my grandmother dragging me around the streets of New York as she panhandled for drinking money. Because of their ignorance of the crafty and manipulative side of my grandmother's alcoholic tendencies, they believed her lies that my mother was neglectful and abusive.

And so, they reported my mother to the police.

This was the last straw for my mom, whose maternal instinct of protection kicked into high gear. Time was up for my grandmother. Phone calls were made, and she was handed off to another relative. But I recognized my mother's pain and regret in doing so.

By the time of the officers' arrival, to follow up on allegations of elder abuse, my grandmother had been evicted. I have no idea what law enforcement threat my mother faced, but I am grateful for her determination to protect me from further harm.

During her stay, my grandmother got a thrill out of knowing she had me at her mercy while my mother was at work. It was my first experience with the bullying and emotionally abusive side of alcoholism.

As I coach families, I find that many of us have similar generational experiences with addicted parents and caretakers. By the time I meet them, they are struggling with a spouse, sibling, or child who is caught in the web of addiction. These situations bring up the past trauma of drunken abuse and neglect from their childhood.

In my experience with my grandmother as my babysitter, my resistance to being placed in unsafe situations was met with a verbally brutal attack. My grandmother knew she held all the power over me. Already struggling with feelings of vulnerability and the uncertainty of childhood, this fear of my grandmother, who I otherwise adored, was truly heart-wrenching.

Her behavior showed me that not all adults could be trusted and that even those who are supposed to love you could do irreparable harm. I think my grandma intended to send me this message as a way of undermining my codependent mother, by testing her love and loyalty as a daughter, and seeing how much she could get away with.

In fact, it was not until I became an adult that I learned of the abuse my mother suffered as she was growing up, as told to me by other family members.

She did everything possible to be the dutiful daughter while harboring great resentment. My grandmother's addiction made her cunning, calculating, and somewhat despicable. But who wants to see their beloved mother in that light?

When my mother confronted my grandmother about putting me in harm's way, my grandmother taunted, bullied, and disrespected her. She dragged her half-paralyzed body to the bathroom, only after waiting until she could no longer hold her movements, relieving herself as she crept across the room, cackling all the way. I was horrified that she challenged my mother in this mean-spirited way, not to mention the shame I felt seeing her in such an embarrassing light.

Of course, when she was not drinking, my grandmother acted as if none of these situations had ever happened. When sober, she was a brilliant conversationalist, highly intelligent, and most charming. But this only lasted until she could coerce an unwitting neighbor to go to the liquor store for her. Sometimes even a stranger.

I loved when she shared stories with me about her childhood in Savannah, Georgia, just after slavery in America was abolished. Unfortunately, the bad times outweighed the good.

But in the coaching work I do now, memories of these experiences help me relate to loved ones trying to understand the same roller coaster of emotional manipulation.

Nothing ever came of the visit from the police. Yet the experience left me with a lingering feeling of fear because of the risk of me being taken away from my single mother. I was relieved by the calm that followed the departure of my grandmother and the chaos she brought with her.

CHAPTER 5

A Tragic Example

My nine-year-old heart ached with the thought of my grieving mother sitting alone at my grandmother's funeral. My mother insisted that I not join her on that night, even when the heavens seemed to weep with torrential rains.

But unbeknownst to her, and for the only time in my life, I experienced a psychic phenomenon. In my heart and mind, I sat quietly by her side in the front row of the wood-paneled funeral parlor. In the days leading up to the funeral, I recognized her regret and her emotional devastation because of my grandmother's passing after a year of estrangement.

Somehow, in my mind's eye, I envisioned the scene as clear as day and wrapped my arms around my mother as she sobbed tears of sorrow and loneliness. After all, I was a living witness to the wasteland of bridges burned and mean-spirited antics that my grandmother used to cut through the lives of so many. Even as young as I was, I understood that sadly, there would be no warm memories or nostalgic words of farewell at her earthly departure.

A little more than a year earlier, my mother packed my grandmother off to the care of the last relative willing to take her in, a cousin in New Jersey. But after just a short while, this cousin, my grandmother's niece who was a nurse, found my grandmother to be too much to handle on her own and had her committed to the hospital psychiatric ward where she worked so she could still keep an eye on her and monitor her care.

Then one day, I came home from fourth grade to find my mother home from work early. She stared out the bay window of our Brooklyn apartment, standing in complete stillness with tears rolling down her cheeks as she peered through the lace curtains, clutching the drapes she herself had tailor-made.

"What's wrong?" I asked, as I slowly approached her, recognizing that something was terribly amiss. After a few minutes of silence, she whispered in words I was barely able to hear, that my grandmother had died.

I joined her in tears, of course, for the death of a beloved one, but with mixed feelings about my grandmother. Yet, as the minutes of silence between my mother and I ticked away, I began to sob uncontrollably, realizing that my mother was so alone in her grief.

Because my grandfather died when my mother was just a toddler, my mother grew up as my grandmother's best friend, especially since she was her only child. She often told me stories of how her mother always took time to play with her when she was young and how close a bond they shared. That is until the progressive disease of alcoholism began its mentally and emotionally destructive course, and my grandmother became mean, bitter, and spiteful.

Because I too was an only child with a special bond with my mother, over the years she recounted some of the painful experiences of living with her mother's addiction. She remembered the ugly words spewed at her, the way her self-esteem was stripped away, the abuse of her loyalty and devotion, and the lying and manipulation.

By the time my mother approached her senior year in high school, she could no longer tolerate the abuse and chose to quit school and move out of town, a decision that had a profound financial impact on the rest of her adult life.

The two were estranged for several years until my grandmother worked her way back into my mother's good graces, only to repeat the cycle of drunken abuse all over again.

Shortly after I was born, my grandmother suffered a stroke which left her partially paralyzed and somewhat of a burden for a working mom with a newborn at home. Thankfully, understanding relatives pitched in and volunteered to take my grandmother in.

Thus began a merry-go-round of evictions and relocations between friends and relatives because of the alcoholic chaos my grandmother brought with her wherever she went. This cycle continued until she landed back with us when I was in the second grade.

At this point, I was at an age to know my grandmother for myself, for the first time.

So, on the fateful day when we got the news of my grandmother's demise, my grammar-school self shared in my mother's regret and sorrow at the ugliness that was, instead of the beautiful mother-daughter-granddaughter relationship that could have been. She lost her mother long before to the personal traumas and wounds that sent my grandmother seeking comfort in a bottle.

But in that moment, there seemed no chance for the sobriety and reconciliation my mother longed for.

The following day, we took the train ride from New York City to my mother's New Jersey birthplace, where arrangements needed to be made. By this point, my grandmother had no financial resources, aside the few dollars the state provided for burial of the indigent. My mother also could not afford much more.

When we arrived at the funeral home to see the body, my heart again ached for my own mother, as she faced the dreadful reality of her mother's loss and financial uncertainty about the possibility of a proper burial.

Fortunately, the owner of the funeral home was a former classmate of my mother's and recognized her situation. As I sat quietly in the office as options were discussed, he assured my mother that he would provide everything for a beautiful service, with no concern for cost.

I remember how in death my grandmother's beauty shone through, and she glowed in peace. This vision of serenity was the grandmother I might have known in sobriety.

The afternoon before the funeral, my mother and I went again to the funeral home to view the dressed body.

True to his word, the funeral director laid out my grandmother in a splendor that exceeded anyone else I have ever viewed. My grandmother looked like an angel with her skin glowing, her hair and makeup perfect, and wearing a beautiful sequined blue gown that highlighted her natural beauty.

She had always maintained her good looks despite years of drinking and a stroke. But in heavenly repose, she looked so alive which brought such comfort to my mother and me.

We discussed as we left how relieved we felt and so grateful to God for his grace. We could see that the person who was so sickened for so much of her adult life was blessed with eternal forgiveness. Finally, her spirit was free of what ailed her.

Still, on the night of the funeral, my mother sat alone in her bereavement, as though my grandmother was all dressed up with no place to go and no one to see her. Not even the niece who cared for her in her final year attended the funeral. It was heartbreaking for me to find out that no one else joined my mother in her darkest hour.

But that was the reality of so many bridges burned over the years. Or maybe the lies spread by my grandmother about my mother.

I'll never know. My older cousin and I sat at her home in almost stunned silence with our hearts weeping, not for the 69-year-old deceased, but for the pain of my mother's unconditional love.

I'll never know why my mother didn't take me along or why she didn't insist that our cousin, who was my grandmother's last caretaker, join her in saying goodbye.

I'm sure the tragic sight of my mother sitting alone was also a painful for the funeral director who was so blessedly kind to his childhood classmate and my grandmother's memory. There was no formal burial service, so I'm sure the next day the funeral home removed the gorgeous gown and reclaimed the expensive loaner casket, replacing it with the cheap one paid for by the state. My grandmother was laid to rest, alone.

The thought of my mother's loneliness compounding her deep sorrow still breaks my heart decades later. It's also a reminder of the shared consequences of addiction. The generational pain.

There's a saying, "If you can't be a good example, be a horrible warning." My grandmother was that warning indeed.

CHAPTER 6

Impeccably Dysfunctional

My dad was a lovely man, but sad and lonely at his core, locked in the prison of alcohol addiction.

He was loved by family and friends, but in a pitying sort of way. Everybody loved being around him when his inebriated humor kicked in, replacing his otherwise sullen demeanor as he struggled through the day without a fix.

Despite his self-acceptance as a "hopeless alcoholic," he always had a "good job," and his personal grooming and appearance were never less than impeccable. He was tall and handsome, with a slender build, light complexion, a V of a receding hairline, and a dimpled chin. We proudly shared the same oval head and face.

My dad never wore jeans or sweats. For work, he wore a shirt and tie. And his casual attire was Dockers with a sharp pressed crease, a buttoned-down collar oxford shirt, stylish socks (usually gifts from me), shined loafers, and a stingy-brim hat. His wardrobe was largely what is described today as business casual.

If he wasn't wearing a sport jacket, one was always neatly folded over his arm. In reality, he was barely functional, but he looked the part of a man who had it all together, except for the shaking hands and liquor on his breath.

As with all addicts, his life was unstable and unmanageable, littered with several marriages, live-in girlfriends, children, stepchildren, and grands.

I only remember him as the sweetest man I've ever known because on the occasions when he saw me, a rare light shone from his eyes and tears welled up. I felt unconditionally loved, though I was aware of his struggle to love himself.

Codependency is a conditioning, a training, a grooming, and a rearing. Conditioning occurs when exposed to this type of relational dysfunction, and the more the exposure, the deeper and more ingrained the traits become. Over time, this training becomes a natural part of who we are. The tentacles of codependent relationships cause the underpinning of families to become shaky and unstable. When we are manipulated and tricked into unhealthy ways of relating to each other, that uncertainty leads to confusion and chaos.

When it came to my father, I was conditioned to be codependent, but not by him. It was my paternal grandmother and mother who did the grooming.

Although my dad never paid child support, whenever I needed something, I could just call him and let him know, whether it was cash or necessities such as clothing or school supplies. Now while he wasn't necessarily dependable in delivering right away, eventually his generous nature could be depended on, especially if requests were made in person when he was intoxicated.

At those times, he was teary and loving, and to my young mind, he seemed to love giving and doing for me. He seemed so sweet and eager while also appearing helpless and vulnerable in his drunkenness. It was as though he was trying to make up for his personal failings. Like he really needed to compensate for his weaknesses and appreciated the chance to do so.

Meanwhile, his mother and mine always schemed on what they could get from him for themselves, by using me. My grandmother, with whom my dad lived off and on when between failed marriages and romantic relationships, always knew when he had extra money coming, such as a tax refund or a bonus from work.

She called my mother to let her know that I should call my dad asking for money or something else that I needed. They encouraged me to ask him to take me shopping, so that I could insist he buy something that they wanted.

I felt so much pressure and deceitfulness for being put in the position to use him this way. Plus, I felt ridiculous asking him to buy undergarments, stockings, or bathrobes for them. I was sure he recognized that he was being played, but to this day, I don't know if he realized the manipulation.

Both women assured me that if my dad was high and feeling good, it was an easy trick to pull off. I was uncomfortable tricking him, but I felt too intimidated by their demands to do otherwise.

I felt sorry for my dad and didn't want him to know that they used me to take advantage of him. It also irked me that they robbed me of the "quality time" that I so wanted to spend with him by forcing me to focus on what they wanted. Not to mention that though he was generous, his financial resources were limited, so what he bought for them took away from what I needed.

What my paternal grandmother and mother actually taught me was how to manipulate an alcoholic and how to take advantage of their weaknesses, compulsions, and distorted judgment.

The longer my dad's absence from my life, which sometimes was months or years, the bigger the opportunity they saw. To their way of thinking, his guilt plus his drunkenness could reap a bounty. They always stressed that I should keep him shopping until his pockets were emptied of everything but lint.

And if he had any cash left at home, I was to ask for it when we returned so that I could give it to my mother and grandmother. They were giddy when tallying up their loot. I only saw how much they took from me while using me in the process, but as I child, I did not feel that my feelings were valued so I kept them to myself.

My father's mother had a glib attitude about his drinking problem, which was common in those days, before addiction was recognized as a disease. She couldn't understand why he wouldn't or couldn't just stop drinking and treated him, in my eyes, as an easy mark.

My mother often told me in private conversation that she couldn't stand my father, but I never saw her treat him with animosity. I knew she viewed him as weak and easy to take advantage of. She seemed mostly dismissive of him because he was the absent parent, which I believe was the reason for her disdain. I defended him in my mind as being sweet and simply misunderstood, but never dared say so out loud.

Though I never knew my parents as a couple because we never lived under the same roof, my dad always showed that he thought highly of my mother, which made me feel safe and loved. Whenever the three of us were together, they were relaxed and comfortable with each other. I appreciated their regard for me in that way.

Of course, my dad didn't openly imbibe during these rare family times. But my mom and I knew he was sipping out of our sight, just enough to keep the shakes down.

I was happy he was in no way the abusive drunk that my maternal grandmother was, so I discounted the effect our dysfunctional relationship had on me. He never created havoc in our lives the way my grandmother did. He was the quiet, mellow drunk. Lovable, and when really feeling good, his sense of humor cracked everybody up. He could be the life of the party, like many people are under the influence when masking their pain

On the days of our father-daughter excursions, my dad started out in a loving and attentive mood. Unhurried but intent on making me happy. But as the day wore on, he'd find ways to discreetly sip from the flask he always carried in the inner pocket of his sport coat.

Meanwhile, my mother and grandmother called his favorite watering holes to let his drinking buddies, my "uncles," know that he would bring me by to show me off, as he always did. It was their job to limit him to one drink and then hustle us off so I would be returned home safely. As I got older, the responsibility of getting home before my dad was too plastered became mine.

In hindsight, my codependent relationship with my dad had a different look and feel than with my maternal grandmother. I did not feel at risk the way she made me feel, and so I trusted his love for me more. I loved and appreciated my dad so much as a person, while also pitying him for his struggles.

He mostly kept his word to me, so I felt I could trust him. But I could see during our visits what a herculean struggle it was for him to ignore the call of the bottle for a little time of normalcy with me. I got the impression that any time spent with his children and stepchildren provided a glimpse of hope that life could be different.

But by the time we parted ways after each visit, a look of personal dejection spread over his face, knowing he was obligated to pour into his mind and body what they needed most.

My father left an indelible mark on me and my life, and I lost him way too soon, having never known him as a sober person.

And since the death of my dad overlapped with the start of my relationship with my future husband, I can only assume that my unconditional love and acceptance of my father, despite his human failings, ensured my willingness to date a man with the same growing problem.

Did I compensate for my dad's loss by starting a dysfunctional relationship with someone new? By holding on to what was familiar to me, yet hoping that circumstances would turn out differently?

Among those who reach out to me for recovery coaching, I rarely meet one who hasn't slipped into a relationship or marriage with the potential to be a repeat of their addictive history with their family of origin.

Dysfunction and codependency are never different. Every day of dealing with an addict, no matter who, guarantees more of the same.

Still, we keep hope alive.

CHAPTER 7

The Look of Love

I'll never forget the look in the eyes of my future husband the day I opened my apartment door to greet him, and we saw each other again for the first time since we were teenagers.

He was no longer the scrawny 14-year-old with the wild afro I first met when we moved from my Brooklyn birthplace to my mother's New Jersey hometown. I was just 13 and starting 8th grade then. But as a native New Yorker, I was quickly accepted by the in-crowd, who was fascinated by my city sophistication.

He was one of the popular boys the girls couldn't stop talking about. He attended a different school, but grew up in the neighborhood, so was known to all my new friends.

When he showed up on my junior high school yard one day, I understood what all the fuss was about.

Already standing at least six-foot-two and exuding all the confident swagger that went with his reputation on the basketball court, I was duly impressed. He was tall, dark, and handsome with long eyelashes that made him irresistibly cute.

I was introduced without any sparks immediately flying because he already had more attention than he could possibly reciprocate from all the other girls. As with all playboys, he offered equal opportunity to all takers. So, when his attention eventually turned to me, we tried "going together" for a couple of weeks. He was used to testing the limits with girls, but when he tried to get fresh with me, he met my street-tough city side, and immediately dumped me.

Meanwhile, his family moved to Pennsylvania, on the other side of the Delaware River, following his parents' divorce. So, his visits across the bridge to the old neighborhood became few and far between.

Years later, when he went off to college, hours away in western Pennsylvania, friends ran into him when he was home for holidays, but he and I never had such chance encounters.

At that time, I lived on my own, working and nearing the end of my college years, too. One day, when my best friend and I were hanging out at my apartment, she told me she had recently seen him and gotten his phone number.

"Let's call him," she said, and so we did.

My 24th birthday was the following week, and upon hearing that news, he asked to celebrate with me. Since, I had no special plans, I invited him over for dinner.

In the week leading up to our reunion, we caught up on the phone, with mostly his boasts about his prowess on the college basketball court.

On the Sunday of my birthday, 10 years after we first met, he stood at my door, a six-foot, four-inch mass of athletic muscle, neatly trimmed afro, full mustache and beard, and those doe-eyed, long lashes.

He was easily recognizable, despite no longer being the pubescent boy I remembered. He was the full-bodied, grown man my friend told me to expect. And he had grown into a real charmer.

The look in his eyes when he saw me was exactly the same, slightly inebriated, loving gaze that my father always greeted me with. The look that lit up my heart every time I saw my dad, who at the time was still alive. Except for the two of them, I have never experienced such a look of unconditional vulnerability, of a pleading to be loved the same way in return. The resemblance was immediate and uncanny.

I was taken aback, somewhat put off by the obvious fact that he had been drinking beer before he arrived. But at the same time, I was flattered that he dug me. I was told by my friend before that day that he was a beer drinker, which was off-putting because of my family history, and I was a teetotaler. But I could tell he wanted to see where our rekindled friendship could go.

He made his intentions clear later in the evening, as he shared with me his grief over the passing of his father just a few months earlier. He sought solace and comfort, but because we were just getting reacquainted, I wasn't sure exactly what I could offer.

What to do? What to do?

As a teenager, I really liked him, although because of his popularity, I hid my feelings behind a mask of girlie ambivalence. Still, because he was the only boy who had ever quit me (I usually did the dumping), I never forgot him.

Somehow, over the years we were out of sight, my infatuation and memories of him lingered. And here he stood, obviously smitten at first sight, a look of the same, silly booziness as my dad on his face.

At the time, I was a single mother, working my way through college. He had recently graduated and was working toward a career.

I did not go to college right after high school because I could not afford to. But I took advantage of the tuition-assistance program offered by the bank I worked for at the end of my senior year in high school and began accruing college credits.

I became financially independent enough to work my way through Rutgers University full-time on scholarships and grants, majoring in Journalism.

He let me know how impressed he was and proud of me, especially accomplishing so much as a single mom. He enjoyed the pot roast I made, saying he was impressed with my cooking skills, too. I was flattered that he was captivated by the woman I had become.

Instead of the impatient, horny, little boy I knew as a teen, he was the perfect gentleman and said good night at the door with a gentle kiss on the cheek. I did not invite anything more.

He lived about 25 minutes away from me in New Brunswick, NJ. So, for the next five years, we maintained a long-distance relationship, spending time together mostly on the weekends, at his apartment or mine.

Although moving close to school might have made my life a little easier, we both agreed from the beginning of our relationship that we did not believe in shacking up. This standard was especially important to me because I had a child. Although we spent time at each other's apartments, we never left a toothbrush, clothes, or any personal items at each other's homes.

While I was uncertain at first about getting into a relationship with him because of his thirst for beer, I was won over by his commitment to such values as not living together before marriage, which I was firmly in agreement with.

Early on, he let me know he planned to marry one day but was dead set against having children before then. He never wanted to disappoint his mother that way. This moral quality really impressed me.

He was never judgmental about me being a single mother and expressed contempt for how my daughter and I were not valued in my previous relationship.

Over the three decades that we were together, my daughter became his own. But still, I was relieved and more than willing to agree never to dishonor him or myself again with an out-of-wedlock pregnancy.

Early on, during one of our nightly phone calls, he told me about a cousin and his longtime girlfriend who loved each other dearly but had a tumultuous relationship. He even acknowledged that alcohol played a big role in their problems. What he said next completely won me over. "Let's be friends and grow from there. Let's not make things complicated with a lot of expectations and demands. Let's just learn to love each other without all that."

In light of my history of difficult and disappointing romances, these words were music to my ears.

In hindsight, I realize there was a subtle message that I did not pick up on about "expectations and demands." I was not to expect or demand that he curtail his drinking. I acquiesced by remaining in denial about a growing problem.

That conversation made it feel safe for me to open my heart and trust. Then and there, I put aside any concerns about the beer drinking, surrendered to his charms, and fell in love.

Thus, began a whirlwind of getting reacquainted with his family, who I knew from the neighborhood when we were growing up. And it wasn't long before he took me to meet out-of-town relatives and friends who were important to his life, including his college teammates and their new wives.

Although both of us worked and lived on our own, we hardly had any real spending money, yet he spent what he could on our dates to restaurants, concerts, sporting events, parties, and weekend getaways.

I chose to ignore the beer can that was always in his hand because he was always happy to be with me. I wanted our time together to be special. Just like when I was with my dad.

About four years into our relationship and a couple years after my college graduation, he put a tiny diamond ring on my finger. I didn't mind the size because it was what he could afford, and we began to plan a bright future together.

What I loved about him was his clarity about what he wanted in life, a professional career, a wife and children, and the American dream of home ownership. Sounded great to me!

By this time, I was too invested in our relationship to insist that he get a grip on his drinking. Actually, I convinced myself that since he only drank beer and never anything hard, there was not much to be concerned about. Especially since he wasn't stumbling around drunk or spending time in bars.

He mostly sat at home during his off time, drinking beer while watching sports. I figured that since I wasn't a drinker, eventually he might ease up.

One day, early in our relationship, he took me home after a fun day spent together, and he asked me to loan him money to buy beer. I flatly refused because I had no intention of supporting his habit in any way. It was the first time I saw his mood turn dark, and a quiet rage boiled up.

There was an uncomfortable silence between us for the rest of the ride. I was definitely taken aback by his reaction but determined to stand my ground. From that day on until the day he passed more than three decades later, he never again asked me to buy alcohol for him, and I never did.

Unfortunately, that was the extent of my boundaries.

Based on my previous dating history, I decided it was best to let him be himself, since he let me be myself. It felt comfortable to be in a relationship of mutual acceptance, which seemed to be the reason we got along so well.

In all our years together, we rarely argued and had only one overnight breakup in our lifetime together. It wasn't until years later, when in therapy, that I learned he seemed so easy going because his emotions were stunted by his drinking.

Because of my family history, I felt any expectations of abstinence from alcohol were pointless. So, I walked into a marriage with a budding alcoholic, eyes wide shut. I hoped for a different outcome, ignoring what I knew from childhood.

On our wedding day, 250 guests from around the country joined the celebration, and I felt happy and blessed. The only downside for me was that my dad was deceased, so he couldn't walk me down the aisle.

Shortly after my reunion with my future husband, my dad passed from the effects of his drinking, combined with diabetes and kidney failure. He had recently remarried and was excited for the future when he was hospitalized for a couple weeks. He died suddenly, just short of his scheduled discharge.

The two most important men in my life never got to meet, but over time, our relationships traveled a parallel course.

Just like my dad always did, my new husband was happy to provide just what I wanted. So, for our honeymoon at a resort in the Pocono Mountains in Pennsylvania, he booked a hotel suite with a heart-shaped jacuzzi. That was all I had asked for. It was the most extravagance we could afford as recent college graduates.

In that tub, I indulged with him in the complimentary Champagne and got quite woozy. But at the same time, I had the sobering thought that I did not want to go down that road with him over the long haul.

Those first wedded years were a balancing act of intimate bliss, budding careers, and domestic teamwork. We were hyper-focused on what we wanted to accomplish in our life together and for our family. Within a couple years, we added a second child and bought a starter home of our own. Our professional lives advanced quickly as he moved into corporate management, and I became a newsroom professional.

In every new marriage, the couple learns things about each other that only come from living together, such as recognizing each other's moods and attitudes, habits, likes, and dislikes. They discover how to overcome disagreements, faults, and weaknesses.

I definitely married a good man with the best of intentions. Unfortunately, despite my family history, I did not recognize the challenges of living with someone who drowned their feelings in alcohol. Someone who was reactive when a simple response would do.

I thought these trials were merely part of getting to know each other on a deeper personal level. Since I grew up with only a passing relationship with my dad, and my grandmother only lived with us for a short time, I did not recognize the personality traits that brewed within my husband.

His growing alcoholism and my budding codependency were past traits we each brought into the marriage.

He never came home from work without first stopping at the liquor store for a six-pack of beer. Over the years, this package became a 12-pack that my mother used to describe as "his briefcase." But since he was not one to hang out in bars and always came straight home, I couldn't complain, although the situation was still not ideal.

He had the usual obsession with sports, typical of many high school and college athletes. And so, when not working, he rarely moved from in front of the television, except to get another beer from the refrigerator. The longer he sat there, the darker his mood got, and any attempt to get his attention was met with an outburst.

When I asked what was wrong, I was always accused of causing problems when there were none. I quickly developed the codependent behavior of not rocking the boat and letting him be. I refrained asking for what I needed, from momentary help with a household chore to a little attention, accepting instead that I asked too much.

Because I felt validated by the outward appearance of my life and marriage, our beautiful children, advancing careers, and lovely home, I minimized my emotional needs.

I figured it was more important for us to get along than for me to stand up to his unreasonable behavior. Thus, I allowed his moods and attitudes to determine my response. Deciding what to say or do based on his potential anger was also a developing trait of my codependency.

Because he did not stagger around drunk, I ignored the alarm bells and the lessons of my family's alcoholism. I convinced myself this time could be different. After all, he was a doting father who couldn't have been more involved in the children's upbringing. He supported the demands of my career, which required me to work nights, weekends, and holidays. And at home, he cooked meals, did laundry, and checked homework.

We enjoyed date nights, had a close network of family and dear friends, and took exotic vacations together for birthdays and holidays. We had annual Christmas parties and summer cookouts that were hot invitations. Our home was always brimming with children and their laughter. His closest friends always chose him as the godfather for their children, so he had six.

All was well, as long as he was not disturbed while sitting in front of the television with beer can in hand.

And then, about 15 years into our marriage, his mother passed, and all hell broke loose.

My in-laws, both his mother and brother, were my constant allies and always expressed bewilderment about my husband's moods and attitudes.

When she was still alive, my mother-in-law occasionally shared with him her concerns about his drinking habits, especially the potential health effects, but mostly let him be. I could always confide in her and depend on her for moral support.

She died six months after a terminal diagnosis, while we were in the planning stages of building our dream home. Its construction took another six months.

When we returned home immediately following her funeral, my husband and I shared an intimate moment between us of consoling and comforting each other by recommitting to our love and devotion.

And while we awaited the completion of our new home, a well-earned dream-come-true that we had worked long and hard to acquire, he seemed to handle his emotional struggles fairly well.

Except he began hanging out in bars with his friends, something he never did before. He stopped at the bar after work, staggering through the door when he arrived home, often in a giggly mood. Sometimes his friends practically carried him to the door, propped him up, and knocked. Then they scrambled to their car to avoid me.

Under the circumstances, I was understanding, recognizing that he was grieving, although I was concerned that his drinking was escalating to hard liquor.

And there was good reason to be to be worried. While I could only recall my grandmother and father at the worst of their disease, I could see the slow and subtle progression of alcoholism burst into full bloom in my husband.

We visited the construction site of our custom-designed new home every weekend. It was a major step up from the fixer-upper that was the first home we purchased two years into our marriage. The excitement always brightened his mood, despite the realization that my mother-in-law wanted to be there for our move in.

But once we moved in without her to share in our joy, my husband became the mean and angry drunk that apparently lurked under the surface of his emotions.

It wasn't until I was driven into therapy by looming marital problems that I learned that years of alcohol dependence had left him without the emotional wherewithal to cope, and so he resorted to what had always worked. Self-medicating.

Our beautiful new home became a battleground where even my codependent approach of appeasement was useless. He began to sleep on the family-room sectional. His separate sleeping arrangement felt like rejection to me, until a therapist told me he was simply staying in close proximity to his alcohol stash. Sure enough, I discovered that he hid airport-size bottles of whiskey throughout the first floor.

We had a German shepherd that he insisted on having bred a few months before we moved. He wanted a full breed with an agreeable temperament, yet even the dog learned to tiptoe around him.

Our lives at home became unmanageable in a way I hadn't experienced since my grandmother lived with my mother and me for those few months.

He stumbled through the door after work each day, angry, critical, and defensive. He found fault with everyone and everything. And I was at a loss of what to do, except to beg him to get a grip on himself and to pray for guidance on how to handle the situation. My therapist explained that I no longer dealt with the man I loved, but with the progressive behaviors of alcoholism.

The best I could do was complain to any and everyone who would listen, seeking sympathy and advice. Friends and family were empathetic and shared my fears for my husband's well-being, but

I'm sure my constant moaning wore on them, for they had no more answers than I did.

The stress of our strained relationship became apparent in my health, as my blood pressure rose from normal to out-of-control, so I let my doctor know about my home situation.

She recommended Al-Anon, which is 12-Step support for family and friends of alcoholics and addicts. As I began attending meetings, I came to understand the disease I was dealing with. There was nothing I personally could do to get my husband's behavior under control.

He still never missed a day of work, although he headed straight to the bar afterwards. But the man who came home was a mean drunk who went out of his way to inflict all of the pain he felt on the family.

By this time, he moved into the executive level of a new company, and over the next five years he took every opportunity to embarrass and humiliate me.

On one such occasion, his company president invited us to join he and his wife and another couple for a Billy Joel concert which we enjoyed from the company box at the arena.

Whenever we went out, I had to be the designated driver, so at dinner in the venue's private dining room, everyone but me shared in bottles of table wine. We traveled by limousine to the arena, and I left our vehicle at the company president's house to join them for the ride.

On the way back from the stadium after the concert, we all laughed and joked in the limo as they resumed drinking, sharing stories of how each couple met. When I chimed in on our story, my husband, in a split second, went from jovial and fun to verbally abusive and combative.

He went into a rage in front of everyone. "What's so funny Gail? You think that's funny?"

I can't even recall what was said, but it was nothing serious. The car went silent as everyone was in shock, and he continued to glare at me and yell. I was so humiliated and everyone else looked on in stunned embarrassment. Even as the conversation started again, the awkward moment was not forgotten.

His public outbursts became a pattern, and it didn't take much for him to scream at me or the kids, no matter where or in front of whom, for reasons we never understood. His unreasonable behavior kept us walking on eggshells.

It became obvious as his weight began to plummet that his health was deteriorating. And because of his family's history of diabetes, my brother-in-law convinced him to see a doctor. Sure enough, he was diagnosed with Type 2 diabetes.

We learned that fluctuations in his blood sugar caused by the excessive drinking were contributing factors to his erratic outbursts. My initial response was relief because I thought this diagnosis would lead to lifestyle changes, but I was sadly mistaken.

He was not yet at the stage of insulin dependence, but since the doctor was already aware of his alcoholism, he was advised that abstinence would be best so that his condition wouldn't worsen. Instead, on the way home from his appointment, he stopped at the liquor store for a bottle of wine.

It was obvious he thought this lesser strength of alcohol was a reasonable compromise, but by the next day, he was back to hard liquor.

Adding to all my emotional upset were memories of how my diabetic father's health declined because he continued to drink, leading to his untimely demise. Family members and friends all joined in urging my husband to get help. Even his college basketball coach and some of his teammates showed up at our door one weekend for a surprise intervention.

He laughed in their faces.

During my desperate calls to doctors and diabetes specialists, I was assured that he would "go down" at some point, and while hospitalized, his drinking issue could be addressed.

So, I clung to this hope, mistakenly thinking that my family's nightmare would soon end.

Except it didn't. And over the next 10 years I traveled down a road of repeated admissions to intensive care, where he was kept alive on respirators, underwent surgeries, or was admitted to drunk tanks.

My deep-rooted codependent tendencies kept me loyal to a fault, believing that I could eventually get control of the situation. I was unwilling to accept the things I could not change. From my childhood experience, I knew where these circumstances were headed, so I prepared myself for the day that alcoholism would claim the life of my beloved. In the end, complications from alcohol addiction, diabetes, and kidney failure did exactly that, just like my dad.

Fortunately for me, I had started the work of my own recovery, faithfully attending Codependents Anonymous meetings, and working with my therapist to prepare for the grief ahead.

As I shared with my therapist my sadness as his health deteriorated, she explained that I had actually been in mourning for my marriage for a long time. This realization allowed me to work through the obvious tragedy I helplessly witnessed from the sidelines and to accept the truth of what was not in my power to change.

At the same time, I faced my emotional challenges with the determination to write a new story for myself. A story that was hopeful and transformative in the face of potential tragedy.

Today, as a certified peer recovery coach, I support loved ones as they write new stories in their own lives, while learning to let their troubled others take responsibility for themselves.

CHAPTER 8

A Progressive March of Self-Destruction

I watched helplessly as my alcoholic husband committed suicide on the installment plan.

Unlike drugs, which can bring a swift and exacting death that is not dependent on frequent use, alcohol seems to pace itself. Its toxic effects march slowly but steadily through the body, feasting first on the brain, the kitchen where it cooks up cravings. Over time, the toxins simmer in the brain as if in a slow cooker.

The younger and less mature the mind and emotions, the more quickly and easily the addiction takes hold. This early onset is what happened in the case of my husband, who I met and developed a crush on at the tender age of 13; he was 14.

By the time he left home for his freshman year of college, he had already developed a taste for beer that never waned throughout his adult life. This thirst became a mainstay of our marital life and that of our children.

Since his alcoholism didn't seem to hinder him from meeting commitments or handling responsibilities, all his relatives and friends, including me, chose to reside with him in denial that he was truly addicted. But one could not help but notice that he was never without a beer in his hand, except during the workday or at places like church.

And although his behavior was somewhat wild and reckless during his college years, especially considering he was a student athlete, upon graduation he was excited about his professional prospects and anxious to take on the responsibilities of husband and father.

However, he was never interested in socializing in a sober environment. And he limited his friendships to those who never questioned his growing consumption habits, which started with a six-pack every evening after work, and eventually grew to a 12-pack a day, and a case every weekend.

For many years, he never appeared to stagger around, never missed work. Still, it became obvious to me over time that there was an inner void he was trying to fill. A trauma he was trying to forget. Childhood wounds he was self-medicating.

From what he shared with me, the spark of his addiction was ignited by his parents' divorce in his early teens. A trauma he acknowledged but was never willing to address.

With every painful life event, such as the death of his father shortly after his college graduation, he turned more and more to his trusted friend, beer. He used alcohol to cope, never openly accepting that he was merely anesthetizing the pain.

Over time, I was emotionally edged out of his heart and mind as the alcohol took up permanent residence. Like a side chick, there was a third party in the middle of our relationship, and I couldn't seem to compete. There is no more desolate feeling then being lonely while in a committed, monogamous relationship.

For me, that commitment was an enormous feeling of being let down and letting myself down, even though I chose to stay. Especially because the emotional abuse and dysfunction became common place as the disease of alcoholism progressed.

But like so many codependents, I was determined to prove my unconditional love and devotion, because from past experience, it was all I knew how to do. When I was a child, with no real influence, I watched from the sidelines as my grandmother and father slipped away.

As an adult, I was not willing to stand idly by as another loved one went down, thinking under these new circumstances I could somehow influence a different outcome.

I couldn't have been more wrong. What experience has taught me, three times over, is that you can't save someone who doesn't want to be saved.

As the beer cans piled up in the recycling bin at our home, my once strapping six-foot-four husband began to wither away, hardly able to maintain a weight of 150 pounds. He ate like a bird as he filled his gut with beer.

Then came the hospitalization for excruciatingly painful attacks of pancreatitis. His body found after years of being fed copious amounts of sugar and yeast-laden beer, it was difficult to produce insulin or digest nutrients.

This illness, I thought, was the break I waited for since he was forced to stop drinking to avoid the pain.

For a short while, I had back the man I first fell in love with. However, because he never sought 12-step support or substance-abuse treatment, his abstinence lasted just long enough for him to pick up old habits again.

He started with non-alcoholic beer, which proved just a new gateway to old habits, since it simply contained a lesser amount of alcohol, but not necessarily enough to create a buzz. The weaker taste drove him back to the higher volume.

I took comfort in the thought that the chronic pancreas attacks would return and force him back to sobriety. But addiction is a sly fox, and he eventually figured out how to drink just enough to satisfy his thirst without awakening the stomach pain of the pancreatitis.

Again, he was off to the races. His addiction became a full-blown problem within a few years of his diabetes diagnosis.

So, while he continued to work every day, surprisingly rising the corporate ladder, he was a totally different person at home, nasty, spiteful, and threatening. There were occasions I had to call the police to keep him from getting behind the wheel of a car while drunk.

My daughters, other family members, and friends were forced to constantly keep tabs on him so that he wouldn't hurt himself or anyone else.

As his weight plummeted and his physique became sickly, we had to trick him into seeing a doctor. His best friend and I tried to gain control by taking him to the emergency room one morning when he staggered too much to resist. There, his doctor admitted him to detox, but within days he checked himself out, tricking a friend to pick him up from the hospital. He went straight to the liquor store for a six-pack.

Of course, his alcoholic mind convinced him not to take heed of any of the lifestyle changes required to survive diabetes, and he continued to spiral downward. Rock bottom was in sight, and I prayed every day that God would do his part to give my husband the wake-up call I thought would solve our problems.

I repeated the Serenity Prayer so many times in Al-anon: "God grant me the serenity to accept the things I cannot change. The courage to change the things I can. And the wisdom to know the difference."

But I was not yet wise enough to know the difference. So, I continued trying to gain control of a situation I had no control of. I was stuck on having the courage to change things beyond my control, namely my husband's desire for a sober life.

It may seem strange to admit, but eventually I could see his rock bottom, as he began to bleed from the mouth for no apparent reason. He even admitted to me that this occurred while he was in executive meetings at work, and it was brought to his attention.

He assured family, friends, and coworkers alike that he was fine, ignoring my insistence that he see his doctor.

In my desperation, I clung to the hope that some consequential circumstance would be severe enough to provoke change. So, I prayed that the rock-bottom opportunity I saw looming would help him understand that his very life was at stake unless he confronted his demons.

I reported the repeated instances of unexplained bleeding to his doctor in a desperate phone call one day, recognizing it was time for medical intervention. She sent an ambulance to our home just as my husband arrived from work and threw himself down on the black, leather, family-room sectional where he drank every night. We were able to get him to the emergency room and he was admitted to intensive care that very night.

The next morning, I got the phone call that I dreaded for so many years.

The attending physician said, "I was talking to your husband this morning while the nurse was washing him up, and he seemed fine until mid-sentence. We lost him."

I gasped in shock, crumbling to the floor before hearing him say, "Luckily, I was standing right there, and we were able to get him back."

My husband flat-lined, but by God's grace and perfect timing, the doctor was there to restart his heart. I was sure this near-death experience was the answer to my years of devotion and prayer.

The diagnosis was pneumatic sepsis; his diabetic immune system was too compromised to fight the consistent alcohol poisoning that took over his bloodstream and filled his lungs. Once resuscitated, he was placed on a respirator to breathe for him while his body detoxed, antibiotics were pumped intravenously into his bloodstream, and the poison was pumped out of his lungs.

I can't describe the initial horror of seeing a loved one hooked up to machines, belching beeps and boops, with tubing taped down their throat, sucking air into their hissing windpipe.

We were 23 years into our marriage, and I felt the sheer terror of not knowing whether he would survive.

After a week, he was brought out of the induced coma, and faced months of recovery and rehabilitation. So debilitating was his condition that he had to learn to walk, function, and care for himself all over again. During the eight months that he was out of work and rehabilitating, he was convinced by doctors to get help, and agreed to attend Alcoholics Anonymous (AA) meetings.

As I was already familiar with the program from my participation in Al-Anon, I took him to his first meeting, which was open to family members. Not all meetings are open.

Meanwhile, the doctors honored my request that he initially be given medication to curb his cravings. They assured me the pills were only effective if taken as prescribed and was only a short-term solution. Still, I was confident that all would be well from now on, and the family dysfunction would come to an end.

I truly underestimated the power of addiction.

Once my husband returned to work, he sought employment in a different company, in a higher, more lucrative executive position. That's when his attendance at AA ended, as his professional success again fed his denial.

For the next 10 years, medical emergencies and hospitalizations became fairly routine. But it's amazing how slick the nature of addiction is, as these episodes always seemed to occur when he was off from work on the weekend, during long holidays, or vacations.

Otherwise, he never missed a day.

During one such episode, we were on a five-hour flight from New Jersey to Cabo San Lucas, Mexico for vacation. Suddenly, my husband slumped over and went into convulsions.

It was a horrifying scene. We were half-way through the flight on an airplane packed with families looking forward to fun in the sun. But there was my husband, bleeding from a portion of his tongue he bit off, his eyes rolled back into his head, and his body stiffened as if jolted by electricity.

In desperation, the shocked flight attendant I summoned to our seats asked for the assistance of any medical professionals on board. An eye doctor and an emergency medical technician answered the call. Looking at his emaciated frame while poking his distended belly, the doctor quickly surmised that my husband had a drinking problem. I also informed them of his diabetes, and they checked his blood sugar to ensure he was not having a diabetic episode, which I initially suspected.

The pilot announced that we had to make an emergency landing in Houston, where ambulances awaited our arrival. We were whisked away, my husband still convulsing and the medical team instructing me to keep up as he was wheeled through the airport.

As we reached the emergency vehicle, I was placed in the front passenger seat as the EMTs worked on my husband in the back for what seemed like an eternity. Once he was stabilized, we were off to a local hospital that specialized in stroke and head trauma, in a city I had never been to before.

I had no idea whether he would live or die this time, no idea where I would stay, and only the clothes on our backs (his had to be cut off him) since our luggage continued on the flight to Mexico.

I granted emergency room doctors permission to place my husband on a respirator (déjà vu all over again) so that he could be kept alive while tests were run. Once this procedure was done, the attending physician found me in the waiting room and got all the pertinent information. Luckily, because of experience, I always kept a list of all my husband's doctors, prescriptions, and medical history in my phone, so I was able to provide the information as immediately needed.

To my total shock, the doctor informed me of the cause of my husband's sudden convulsions. They were caused by an addiction-related condition I was unaware of, alcohol-withdrawal seizures.

Although my family and I had not seen my husband drink in a while, that didn't mean he was sober. We now realized that his drinking was just less obvious to us. In fact, while he traveled on business, which was often, and spent time at the

72

country club where membership was a perk of his executive job, he apparently indulged regularly.

But being sober as we travelled that day, his brain went into shock when its dependency was not fed in more than 24 hours. I now know why addicts must withdraw under medical supervision. Withdrawing cold turkey can be fatal.

The next shock was learning that my husband had to be hospitalized for more than a month as he was kept stable during the necessary detox.

This incident happened at the start of the Memorial Day weekend, so the car rental agencies were closed until the following Tuesday, and I was without transportation. I had no idea where I could stay.

After calling our family back home to inform them of this latest emergency, with the guidance of an emergency room nurse, I was able to book a room at a hotel just down the road that offered shuttle service to and from the hospital. Once I settled in, I immediately went to work, contacting the employee assistance program of my husband's employer, explaining the emergency, and asking for help.

By day's end, they got approval for his admission to an inpatient alcohol and drug rehab with a stellar reputation right there in Houston. A bed was waiting for him upon his release from the hospital weeks later.

I appreciated the privacy and confidentiality guaranteed by employee assistance programs and HIPAA laws because I did not know whether my husband's company was aware of his drinking problem.

As far as I was aware, they only knew of his struggle with diabetes, information he shared as a way to excuse signs of his drunkenness. He explained his behavior away as having a blood-sugar episode. When a diabetic's levels are dangerously high, they sometimes act irrationally and have violent outbursts. This made for a convenient explanation for his behavior sometimes.

By the end of the first week, my husband was kept alive on machinery in the Intensive Care Unit. The doctors stabilized him enough to awaken him from another induced coma. In the following weeks, he was kept under 24-hour-a-day seizure watch and went in and out of hallucinatory and delusional episodes.

I was too disappointed and resentful to spend long days in the hospital. I also was not willing to tolerate the verbal and emotional abuse that came with his detox.

Still, it took a lot of nagging and cajoling on my part to get the hospital's medical and social services staff to agree to release my husband into rehab there in Texas. They tried to convince me to take him home and have him admitted to a facility there, something I knew he would never agree to.

I knew he needed to be away from home, work, friends, and his familiar environment so he could focus solely on his sobriety to the exclusion of all else. I also didn't feel he was physically strong enough for a flight home, which made me nervous about the possibility of another frightening crisis on the flight back.

By the fourth week of my husband's hospitalization, I convinced the doctors and social worker to explain to him how life-threatening his alcoholism was. They strongly suggested that he take advantage of the opportunity for treatment that was already arranged.

He reluctantly agreed. I was optimistic, but past experience told me not to get too excited. Still, I felt the end of the long nightmare of his alcoholism was within sight. How many brushes with death did he need to recognize his rock bottom? Surely, this situation was as low as he would be willing to go.

I couldn't have been more wrong.

After two weeks in rehab, he checked himself out, and his alcohol counselor told me that this decision would cost him his life.

It took another five years of deteriorating health, medical emergencies, and finally job loss before her prognosis became reality.

Lucky for me, his repeated stints at rock bottom were enough to get me to finally understand the

Serenity Prayer for myself. What I knew for sure was that the only thing I could change was myself.

And with that realization, I did just that.

CHAPTER 9

My Road to Recovery

When I appeared at the therapist's office for an orientation session, I was shaky and unsteady on my feet. It was about a week after the fateful morning of my mini breakdown, and I was required to go so that the right counselor could be assigned for me.

My husband and I had been married for 28 years, and I was still trying to keep my family together, although looking back, I'm not sure why. Maybe it was that I remembered my mother's heartache because of her estrangement from my grandmother before her death. I was also concerned about what other people would think if I abandoned my husband.

This self-defeating worry is something I counsel families in my coaching program to avoid. Other people may judge and have opinions, but they're not walking in our shoes, and can't understand our pain. These situations call for professional advice.

This reality I knew for sure as I stepped into the therapist office. My mind was clouded by shame and resentment, but my spirit was desperate for relief.

My husband had checked out of rehab despite another near-death experience. I had no idea where my life was headed, I just knew I was out of hope.

I looked at the modest brick building, formerly a private residence on a quiet, mixed commercial and residential street, wondering whether it held any answers inside. Could the peace I so desperately yearned for, over more than a decade, truly be found inside this aging, converted abode?

I drove slowly down the side driveway and felt lucky to find a parking space in the row of only four lined spots, in the rear of the building, next to an old garage. I was glad that the entrance was in the back of the building, mostly invisible from the street, so that I could not be seen by a passerby who might recognize me. I wanted the comfort and protection of confidentiality.

I slowly opened the door, peering inside with hope, hesitation, and expectancy. I needed to acclimate myself to this new environment, where I would share my most private thoughts and feelings.

The receptionist was friendly enough and got on with the first order of business which was checking to see if my insurance plan covered my therapy. Once it was determined that it would, the next step was filling out the requisite forms with my personal information, physician contact information, and medical background.

Taking care of these business particulars gave me a chance to ease into the process. It felt like a routine doctor's visit.

I wasn't sure how to answer questions about my mental health, but I included my doctor's diagnosis of traumatic stress. Acknowledging this condition was jolting to me, because I had only previously heard it applied in cases of soldiers returning from war zones.

Lord knows, I lived in one for many years.

But I also had to admit that traumatic stress was an accurate assessment of what I felt: traumatized, demoralized, and angst-ridden.

Up until that point, I had lived my life in avoidance, trying not to think about the possibility of another medical emergency. Fearful of the next assault on my heart and emotions. I felt that the insanity of alcoholism I lived with enveloped my mind as well, like a virus infecting my brain.

I went through the motions of my life half-heartedly, struggling to find contentment in activities I once loved. Whatever freelance projects I took on, I couldn't seem to fully enjoy. The sense of achievement I experienced from my work was minimal. And dealing with other people felt like a chore.

I spent long hours at night at my computer, trying to write and be creative, but with no real motive or results. My thoughts were muddled, and I was unfocused.

I had trouble going to sleep at night and difficulty waking up until late in the morning. I hardly ever cleaned my house and spent my days immersed in mindless distractions, such as hours of watching television, shopping, or going to the movies.

Although I always participated in fitness classes of some sort, from step classes and aqua aerobics to gym workouts, these were mostly desperate attempts to lose weight and to feel a sense of purpose. But I could never seem to lose the weight, even when attending Weight Watchers meetings.

Even though I made some progress with my blood pressure and insulin-resistance issues, my outer body was a true reflection of my inner being. The toxic dysfunction of my family life was evident in my appearance.

In reality, I was just tired of walking on eggshells when home alone with my husband. So, I was always looking for something productive to do to stay out of sight.

I downloaded hours of hip hop and R&B music into my iPod and plugged in my headphones, bopping to the music for hours, in a futile attempt to lift my spirits.

I also struggled to believe in something beyond my social status and the affluent lifestyle we built over more than two decades of marriage. I longed for a personal significance beyond my roles as wife and mother. These parts were just reminders of my dysfunctional and codependent life.

Meanwhile, I still played the dutiful corporate wife role, going to dinners at the country club where my husband had membership as a perk of his executive position, and traveling with him on business trips, during which I hosted or was hosted by other executive's wives.

It was just as important to me as to my husband that we keep up these professional appearances. Yet, he told me that having me by his side really did not add value to his corporate life. His statement was insulting, confusing, and especially hurtful since the other executives seemed to truly appreciate having their wives with them and getting a chance to socialize together during business gatherings.

Although he would never admit it, I know that even the vacations that we took, such as the trip to Cabo San Lucas, Mexico that had to be aborted because of my husband's medical emergency, provided a front for the image he portrayed in the corporate world of a thriving marriage and happy family life. His denial of his alcoholic dysfunction ran deep and so did my codependency.

We both hid the ugly truth behind appearances.

I wanted our marriage to match the outward appearance of our life together, with all the material abundance, financial affluence, and career accomplishments. I believed in the dream but lived the nightmare. My husband always insisted that we had the dream in the palm of our hands, and all I needed to do was enjoy it. He couldn't understand why I felt so unfulfilled in our life together.

The truth was, I knew that being married to a man who for years was stuck in self-destruct mode could never feel fulfilling or worthwhile. Living a paradox could never be healthy. Instead, it led me to a nervous meltdown after his early exit from rehab, and a trip to a therapist's office to seek help and healing.

Even though my husband turned down a chance for rehabilitation, I realized that I wanted treatment. I was willing to do whatever was necessary to restore my health and sanity.

So, there I sat, in a cramped back room, seated on a well-worn and sunken cloth-covered couch, talking to an intake counselor who would determine which therapist was best to pair me with. It was an all-female practice, which was my preference, when given the choice by the benefits program.

"So, what brings you here," the intake counselor asked. "How can we help?"

I immediately launched into the whole sordid story, starting in reverse chronological order with my husband suffering seizures on the plane. I relayed his long history of alcoholism and near-fatal medical emergencies, his admission to rehab and insistence on early discharge, and the subsequent nervous breakdown that I suffered.

She listened intently, nodding her head with understanding, her facial expressions showing concern and empathy. She also seemed especially familiar with my story, having heard similar versions many times before.

As the end of our scheduled hour approached, she seemed both knowing and excited about the possibility of providing help. I really didn't know what to expect, since in the past I visited with therapists who only listened as I vented about my husband. They gave me insight into the alcoholic mind and personality, but never gently nudged me into recognizing my own role in my suffering and willingness to stay in the situation.

My initial attempts at counseling were in the early years of my husband's spiraling, and I was mostly advised to join an Al-Anon fellowship, which I did.

But I sometimes found the sharing to be more depressing than hopeful. I felt the philosophy was one of acceptance and powerlessness, and simply learning how to cope through Bible readings and prayer.

I was already stuck in a white-knuckle approach to muddling through my relationship. So, for me, the meetings felt disappointing and depressing. I did, however, embrace a morning routine of daily readings from the books we used in the program, in a desperate attempt to understand my husband's alcoholism.

I seriously contemplated each day's reading in order to get my bearings.

Over the years that I maintained this routine, I gained clear insight into the roots of my husband's drinking problem, the effects of the disease on his nervous system, and his denial and fear of sobriety. What I didn't find were any answers that explained me. There was no real explanation or understanding of codependency. In fact, I never read any reference to it at all.

But as I sat in the nearly claustrophobic intake office at the new counseling center, desperate for help, I had no idea that I was at exactly the right place to get the help I needed.

In a few days I received a call and was given the name of the therapist who would work with me, and an appointment was made.

Since the initial referral was through my husband's employee assistance program, which also helped me get him into rehab, there were no co-payments for the first six sessions. In this situation, I knew it was important to take advantage of any health and wellness benefits available to me, because my life and emotional well-being were at stake.

When I showed up for my scheduled appointment, I was a little taken aback by the open waiting room, where all the clients sat together waiting to see their individual counselors. This setup was very different from my previous experiences with high-end psychologists, whose offices had private waiting rooms and building exits designed to preserve the privacy of their patients.

I sat nervously with other clients, hoping that no one I knew would come through the door. I was relieved that it never happened but found the few minutes that my counselor took to finish up with the previous consult a bit unnerving.

My therapist was just the opposite of me in a lot of ways. We were both overweight, but she was short and plump, while I was tall and leaner in appearance. She was white and brunette, and I, an African American with reddish blonde hair.

She looked like the typical middle-class, suburban wife and mother, with a casual style of dress, and a sunny, smiley demeanor that matched her physique. My style was decidedly hip and urban.

As we climbed the stairs to her small office in a former bedroom on the second floor, I was unsure if she could even relate to me or my experiences.

Once inside her private space, she let me choose which of the chairs facing each other that I wanted to sit in, with a window air conditioner between us to combat the July heat. Coincidentally, I did not choose the seat that was actually hers.

As we sat face to face, I explained my reason for being there, and the near-tragic event on the plane to Mexico that was the catalyst for my breakdown.

Over the course of our sessions together, she shared personal information with me, such as her upbringing in Newark, long known as a gritty city in north Jersey, famous for some of the worst riots of the 1960s, which was followed by white flight. She also confided that she had a severely handicapped child with special needs which required her to have flexible work hours and a job close to home.

This child, who was one of two siblings, was now in school, which made life a little easier for her as a working mother.

By sharing these tidbits about her personal life and our common urban roots, she put me at ease, and we were able to develop an easy rapport.

Eventually, she convinced me that I had to talk about my husband and his problem drinking before we could determine what I could do to heal from the personal trauma of the situation. I had hoped not to rehash all the painful details because my story was my main topic of conversation with all who would listen for so long.

But she was right; she needed to be brought up to speed about how the situation spiraled so out of control that I collapsed under the weight of it all.

As I rehashed incidents of verbal and emotional abuse and public humiliation, she explained how the alcoholic mind is always reactive and never simply responsive. The toxic effects of alcohol on the brain often causes them to react with verbal outbursts when a simple statement or response would be more appropriate.

This pointed explanation helped me understand that I bore no blame for his behavior in these situations. I also had no control over his words or actions because he, himself, lacked the awareness of why he said and did the things he did. He was essentially powerless against his disease.

These clarifications relieved me of some of the personal blame and resentment that I felt toward my husband. They actually helped me develop a measure of empathy and compassion.

Next, she helped me understand the importance of establishing firm boundaries so that I would no longer tolerate the abuse.

In Al-Anon, I learned that engaging in arguments, making demands, or issuing ultimatums were all futile attempts at forcing change or trying to get control of the situation. There was no way to win against the devious nature of the disease of alcoholism.

But my new counselor helped me see it was possible to make clear what I would or would not tolerate without getting caught up in arguments, screaming, hollering, demanding, or pleading. I began to understand that I didn't have to accept verbal or emotional abuse. She gave me some wording to use as tools in such situations to help maintain those boundaries.

I began to recognize my years of accepting bad behavior and victimization. I just needed the right tools to regain my peace of mind.

I had long had an interest in meditation, but was discouraged from the practice by my mother, who believed such things were satanic and would lead only to an eternity in hell. But once I learned to trust my intuition and saw the benefits of dropping childhood indoctrinations, I told my therapist of my curiosity.

Although a staunch Catholic who did not practice meditation, she was somewhat versed in present-moment mindfulness and encouraged me to investigate further. She saw no harm in trying any tool that brought me peace of mind.

Shortly thereafter, I saw a flier on a bulletin board at my local community center for an Introduction to Meditation meeting, so I attended with a friend. A small group of about 20 people gathered in a classroom at a local synagogue. Our ages and reasons for being there varied widely.

However, throughout the hour-long talk, the short, balding instructor, a college psychology professor, seemed distracted and tentative, even while leading an initial meditation. My friend and I surmised that he was rehashing in his mind an argument he had with his wife earlier that day, or maybe he just had a bad day at work. One thing was for sure. Meditation didn't seem to help him stay in the moment at all.

The professor offered an eight-week course of group instruction, but I knew he was not the one to steer me where I wanted to go.

I advise anyone going through these personal trials to seek the therapist, support group, coaches, and programs that are a right fit for you. If one doesn't meet your personal needs, keep looking, and you will find a good fit. Just don't give up.

Even though my therapist had no experience with meditation as a therapeutic tool, she continued to encourage any steps I took toward healing. She graciously gave me her personal cell phone number and scheduled me in whenever times were tough. We found ways to work around the payment limitations of the medical insurance, and I so appreciated her commitment to my well-being.

After just a couple months, during which I began to gain true insight into myself, I learned of an emotional healing retreat at the spiritual center founded by Deepak Chopra just outside San Diego. I withdrew money from my personal accounts and bought a plane ticket.

I had never spent so much money before to attend any type of workshop or conference, but I was willing to explore any for restoration of my peace. I was willing to go anywhere to seek answers. And where better to learn meditation? My counselor was thrilled for me and complimented my initiative.

The Chopra Center is set in a lush, gated resort and golf course off the Pacific Coast Highway. All along the highway, there were signs for all varieties of sanctuaries offering instruction and comfort in Eastern philosophy. I was awed by the beautiful surroundings, posh gardens, and rolling green hills surrounding the Chopra Center, just a short distance from the Pacific Ocean.

Because of Chopra's name recognition and my own desperation for healing, I bought a couple of Deepak's books. One in particular was on meditation and recovery.

From my reading, I accepted that meditation was a beneficial tool for rebirth and healing. In fact, I was so sure that I would gain new perspective, and more importantly peace of mind at the retreat, that I purchased a first-class plane ticket for the five-hour flight back home, to treat myself.

I was certainly not disappointed by my time at the retreat, and thus started my journey of enlightenment and self-awareness. The yogis and meditation instructors at the Chopra Center are the most calm and centered beings I ever met. There were never any lectures nor stern, raised voices preaching at us. It was just the comforting environment I needed.

Every day, we sat in a small auditorium, facing the low stage where a medical doctor and certified meditation instructor spoke to us about life in quiet, calming tones.

The first topic of discussion was limiting beliefs, a concept that was brand new to me. That moment is when the window to my life opened for me. I realized I had so many limiting thoughts that were ingrained in me from childhood, especially from my religious upbringing.

I believed that God was sorely disappointed in mankind and was sitting in wait to show his displeasure by punishing us for our bad behavior.

While meditation is not a religious practice but a spiritual one, I had room to examine my heart and know that such a belief in a God of harsh judgment could never provide peace and comfort.

I also came to see prayer in a new way. While I was raised to plead with God for what I wanted and needed, I came to understand that the Universe already holds all the abundance we need. Meditation offers the chance to listen to the Creator rather than talk at him. Sitting in silence allows me to hear the "still, small voice" of intuition and spiritual direction that I needed.

I also began journaling, something I always wanted to do but seemed no good at, despite being a writer. But at the Chopra Center I was given guidance and prompts that allowed me to write about my beliefs and then read them back to see if they served me.

I found out that many of the principles I was raised with only led me to feel unlucky, unappreciated, and victimized. These beliefs became the reality of my life. These feelings became self-fulfilling prophecies.

I came to understand that by changing my perceptions and personal outlook, I could make new choices and write new chapters in my life that reflect my desires. Yet, at the time, besides an end to the abuse, pain, and loneliness, I didn't even know what I truly desired for my life.

To find the answer and true peace of mind, I approached my life like a demolition and reconstruction project, emptying my inner self of old attitudes and habits, while building a firm spiritual foundation of meditation, prayer, and journaling.

My outer shell, I redesigned with Zumba and Yoga. Before long, the weight began to fall away, and my general health improved dramatically. I realized that during all the previous years of working out, I aimed for change from the outside in. But when I started working from the inside out, real differences began to show.

I recognized the benefits of my own personal recovery immediately. Physically, mentally, emotionally. And the best was yet to come.

Part 2

My Recovery

CHAPTER 10

Healing and Rebirth

I left the Chopra Center with lessons and tools for my healing from years of codependent trauma. My starter kit was a daily practice of meditation, journaling, and prayer.

While there, we started each morning with yoga and meditation. These sessions were accompanied by soothing, sacred music played by a harpist. It was such a calming way to start the day. No hustle or bustle. Nowhere to be. Nothing to do but be present in the moment.

Because of my years as a journalist, my daily routine previously started with flipping on the television as soon as I opened my eyes from the night's sleep and focusing immediately on the morning news. It was my job to stay abreast of the world's war zones, both on the battlefield and in the political and business arenas, crime, justice and injustices, sports, entertainment, and the weather. I wanted to know everything I learned about in my college journalism major at Rutgers University that the citizenry had a right to know and was fit to print.

I prided myself on always being in the know. Over time, however, I became disillusioned about why it was important to stay abreast of all the ugliness in the world, since despite the constant flow of information, not much seemed to change.

In the sacred atmosphere at the Chopra Center, I came to understand that by feeding my day on an emotional breakfast of death and human despair, I infused my nervous system with stress and anxiety before I even said good morning to my family and coworkers. No wonder I was so cranky in the morning. I struggled to get my mental and physical engine revved up and fought fatigue even after a full night's sleep.

In contrast, every activity at the Chopra Center began with a period of meditation, of quieting the mind and spirit. I learned not to struggle with my thoughts, but instead focused on a mantra that was assigned specifically to me.

By being open to the experience, I was introduced to my inner self. I discovered the heart center of intuition and knowing, just by sitting quietly and breathing in the comfort of either sacred sounds or complete silence. I found that this practice is not religious, but is life-changing if practiced religiously, which is exactly what I have done in the years since.

Prayer is talking to God, while meditation is listening.

For years, I had begged and beseeched the heavenly powers to awaken my husband, to no avail. But at last, I was quiet enough to hear my Higher Power speaking to me.

While taking these baby steps into the unfamiliar, I heard this universal power encourage me to look within myself because the answers I was seeking could not be found by changing another, but only by making changes in me.

Love, respect, comfort, caring, and healing were always available to me without asking, but until that moment, I was not fully aware that these were gifts I could give myself. That I did not have to depend on another for these needs to be met. I could trust my inner guidance, my intuition, to lead me to freedom.

It became a joy to awake each morning, not to a television blaring news of catastrophe and chaos, but to the still small voice of peace, hope, and healing.

The next powerful tool in my kit was a daily journal, where I began chiseling away at the limitations of my parental, religious, and social conditioning. These old beliefs taught me that suffering and womanly self-sacrifice were virtuous. I used my journal to take inventory of these limiting beliefs through free expression of my heart and soul, to empower myself.

After my morning silent time to listen to my Higher Power, I put pen to paper to detail the whispers of my inner guidance. These writings helped me see that I surrendered power over my own life by choosing my own victimization. But finally, I realized I could take my power back.

I saw that contrary to what I was taught at home, in school, and in church, there was no honor in being a people pleaser, of overextending myself for others while ignoring my own needs, of tolerating abuse, and not insisting on being treated as I deserved. I determined that I would stop saying yes to what I didn't want, just to please someone else. I had the right to say no.

The more I examined the true desires of my heart, the steelier my determination became to set firm boundaries of self-respect around my life.

As the weeks went by, I reviewed some of my previous journal entries and uncovered some saddening realities. I realized just how emotionally hardened I had become from my lifetime of trauma and disappointments.

As I shed the weight of continuing abuse with these self-revelations and surrendered the pain to my Higher Power in meditation, I released fear and embraced self-love through a daily deluge of liberating tears that were like chicken soup for my ailing heart.

The initial days of grief and sobbing turned my mourning into gladness for new life and the rebirth of my spirit. My future looked hopeful because I saw no need to blame another. I took the reins of my own life back into my hands.

It wasn't long before the rain gave way to sunshine, and I saw a rainbow over the horizon of my life, accepting new possibilities for myself apart from the choices my husband made for himself.

It was not easy to release some of the more pious teachings from my childhood, such as my unworthiness of God's love, and the need to be saved from myself. Because of my past experiences, how could I not feel at a disadvantage in life from this early indoctrination? That struggle and strife were the natural order of human existence? That life was against me and not for me?

Because of such beliefs, I accepted my family situation as an expected part of life's trials. The rightful outcome of humankind's sinful nature and God's punishment. I thought, even as a child, that I was destined to pay a price for the sins of the world. Still, I didn't understand what my innocent self did to deserve these traumatic life circumstances. Life seemed so unfair.

As I began my recovery journey, I dared to reject these beliefs that led me to a lifetime of fear, doubt, self-sacrifice, and displaced loyalty. I opened myself to new possibilities for happiness and freedom.

At our lowest points in life, we reach out to God to pull us through. Yet, I had learned to approach the Divine from a place of fear and judgment, as opposed to eternal and unconditional love.

Through my recovery, I looked beyond the teaching of a God that resided outside of me and embraced the Higher Power that lived within and was always available in the quiet of my listening.

I decided to be true to the still small voice within, rather than the perceptions of the world without.

I filled my journal with pages and pages affirming my worthiness. I replaced blame and shame with acknowledgements of grace and gratitude.

I took stock of all the ways I dishonored myself by accepting bullying, emotional assault, anger, and humiliation at the hands of so-called loved ones, when as an adult, I didn't have to. I poured my anguish, blame, and embarrassment onto the pages of my journal. I forgave myself and declared my freedom.

I no longer saw my human vulnerability as an excuse for accepting mistreatment just because my abuser was impaired by substance abuse. And I refused to allow disrespect for any other reason, for that matter.

I wrote and accepted my innermost thoughts and feelings as legitimate and valid whether or not they were agreed upon by others. I came to terms with my confusions, doubts, and fears, acknowledging they merely represented opportunities for personal growth. In my journal, I dug deep down in my heart to retrieve remnants of self-love from my tattered soul, and I restored my emotional health.

My journal is where I painted a new soul profile of myself, leaving the past behind with no regrets but only gratitude for the lessons learned. I recognized a new me in the mirror of my present and future, with a more optimistic outlook on life. I granted myself forgiveness and compassion for the self-love I had lost.

The third tool in my recovery kit was two-pronged: prayer, starting with a true understanding and appreciation for the Serenity Prayer; and the spiritual community of 12-step fellowship, church, and any community offering like-minded soul support.

During my initial involvement with Al-Anon, I was motivated by my frustration with my husband's need to get help, and so I didn't come to terms with my personal need for help.

Actually, I was still so focused on him that I resented going to meetings, which I find to be a common sentiment among those that I coach. It's a corner I help them turn, because 12-step membership or spiritual community guards against feelings that each of us struggles alone. These communities provide the loving and caring support of camaraderie.

At the same time, the daily sacred practice of prayer, to whatever higher power one claims, fortifies the heart and mind against falling back into old patterns.

Through these practices I discovered the golden key of recovery: Awareness.

Awareness of self. And awareness of the power of personal transformation that we all possess.

Awareness of an ever-present power that resides within us all and helps us overcome trying circumstances. Awareness of a spiritual answer to earthly problems.

Awareness = Recovery.

CHAPTER 11

Recovering My Lost Self

My diagnosis of post-traumatic stress was an eye-opener for me, both life-changing and life-affirming. A true blessing in disguise because this prognosis called me to discover myself and get clear about who I was and what I wanted.

As I returned home from the Chopra Center, I was determined to heal from the trauma of my life experiences, despite my husband's decision not to get outpatient treatment or 12-step support.

Through my journaling, I affirmed that I would no longer walk on eggshells for fear of upsetting him. I recognized that I was conditioned to tiptoe around my loved ones and their problems since childhood.

I wanted to be healthy and happy, knowing it was what I deserved and trusting the tools I now had to tap into my inner strength. It was time to discover myself and to embark on reinvention.

As I continued to meet weekly with my therapist, she helped me forgive myself for my willing self-sacrifice. She encouraged my steps toward a new future, shifting my focus from pleasing others to self-preservation.

During this time, I continued to research issues of family dysfunction and recovery. In doing so, I discovered the book *Codependent No More,* by psychologist Melody Beattie, a recovering codependent largely credited with coining the phrase.

Beattie is one of the first to share her life experience with how family ties to addiction warped relationships and led to codependency. The book is widely viewed as the bible on the subject.

As I read Beattie's personal account, I felt she was telling my story, too. And I came to see what ailed me and brought me to the verge of a full-blown nervous breakdown.

I finally understood how I accepted the string of alcoholic loved ones in my life as part of my birthright. I always felt fortunate that I personally was not afflicted with the disease, despite the possibility of a genetic predisposition. But I was never aware of how I shared in the illness of my family since childhood.

As the author outlined what she eventually learned about herself, the seed of understanding recovery was planted in me.

A lifetime of unhealed trauma and familiarity led up to a predictable outcome and set of behaviors. I learned to be loyal to a fault, enabling my family in their alcoholism, and quick to make excuses for them, all codependent traits.

These issues were all symptoms of relational illness and dysfunction. With this new awareness, I knew I need not suffer any more.

I relayed this discovery to my therapist, who was not familiar with the term codependency itself. But she understood the concept all too well and supported me in my decision to switch from Al-Anon to Codependents Anonymous (CoDA).

She and my doctor recommended the fellowship Adult Children of Alcoholics, but at the time, I didn't connect my immediate problem to my family of origin, mostly because my grandmother and father were never permanent residents in my home during my childhood.

That understanding would come later.

A simple Google search led me to a local 12-step CoDA fellowship. Nowadays, there are 12-step programs for every type of addictive or emotional disorder, from gambling, grieving, and shopping addiction to eating disorders. I recommend these support systems to all my clients.

In the small, comforting CoDA community of fellow travelers and the safe space of anonymity, my self-discovery deepened.

When I first read the list of traits of codependency, it was like looking in a mirror the morning one wakes up with a hangover. What I saw looking back at me was not pretty, and this new awareness was downright sickening.

The short list of codependency traits included a need to control situations and other people, self-sacrifice, remaining loyal and tolerant to a fault, people pleasing, always going along to get along, putting the feelings of others ahead of one's own, and insisting on taking care of others, even when not asked.

Over the decade that my husband's drinking spiraled out of control, I was guilty of all this behavior, but thought I was simply keeping my family together.

But I finally realized that these personality traits, among many others, are at the root of codependency. This base is why it's also referred to as co-addiction.

I couldn't believe the role I played in my own shame, blame, and resentment. How I made my husband's problem the focus of my life and futilely pinned all my hopes for future happiness on his willingness to get help. I placed my need to protect him from himself over my own mental and emotional self-care. I realized how I tied the quality of my life to the quality of his.

While my emotional needs were left unmet because of his drinking, I suffered in silence and was disloyal to myself. Even though I followed my own interests and passions, I endured feelings of abandonment and isolation in my marriage.

With these new revelations, I embraced the changes that could set me free. As awareness leads to recovery, recovery leads to change.

I came to understand that I would benefit most from my own transformation, whether my husband chose recovery for himself or not.

Ironically, change is often what addicts and codependents alike fear most.

Acknowledging the need for help and change takes great courage. And for those in the grips of codependency, it is often more difficult to recognize the need for personal transformation because of our stubborn desire for our loved one to change.

Because of our insistence on trying to control a dysfunctional situation, we believe, to our own detriment, that our lives would be better if only our loved one would get help. And this point might be true, except the choice is theirs alone to make. We have no control over their choices.

We can only control our own actions, attitudes, and behaviors. It's up to us to recognize our own self-harm in the situation and to do something about it. Addiction is a family disease, and recovery is for everyone involved.

Even if your loved one chooses to accept rehab, family recovery is a two-way street. And if, as a codependent, we must make the trip to recovery alone, then that we must. With the support of therapy, fellowship, and spiritual community, we need never walk alone.

CHAPTER 12

Codependent Reflection Staring Back at Me

I pulled my car into the parking lot of the suburban strip mall, trying to figure out where the Codependents Anonymous meeting I found through a Google search might be.

According to the meeting notice, the fellowship met behind the tire store that stretched the full length of one side of the shopping center. I pulled around back, where all I saw was the dingy rear of retail shops, not intended for public view.

But on the other side of the parking lot, on a grassy, curbside patch off the lined parking spaces, I saw a small gathering of four or five people seated in a circle on white plastic lawn chairs.

How discreet was this meeting place, I asked myself? But I decided to park and approach, putting my anonymity on the line as I asked if I had found the correct group. Yes, I had.

It was a beautiful midsummer evening, with mild temperatures and the approach of a setting sun, so the group decided to risk being made a meal by mosquitos and held the meeting outdoors instead of in the confines of the nearby meeting room. As the meeting time neared, a few more people joined.

The first time at a new 12-step meeting is always awkward, sort of an admission of desperation. But my trepidation has always been met with knowing smiles and a glad welcome. All such fellowships adhere to a similar order, and everyone introduces themselves by first names only.

Beyond that generalization, I must keep my commitment to confidentiality and state that this recounting is about my personal experience only.

The first thing I learned was that codependency means losing oneself in relationships with other people, be they parents, children, spouses, lovers, or friends. We surrender our power to these relationships in search of love, acceptance, or personal validation.

Some of us are born to situations that shape us into codependency, through a dysfunctional family of origin or even to parents who were raised as codependent unknowingly, because it's a fairly new way of looking at survival patterns in relationships with addicts. Codependency is sometimes referred to as the "dis-ease of the lost self."

As the meeting started and we read out loud the traits of codependency, I was blown away in discovering the many ways I had betrayed and lost myself, a necessary admission for recovery.

During my weekly attendance, I discovered that I was deeply wounded by my childhood experiences in ways I never realized. I rarely felt safe in relationships with others, which is a common trait for those who have lived in the chaos of a loved one's addictive behavior.

Codependents tend to be hyper-vigilant, never knowing when the unexpected might happen, such as an angry outburst or verbal abuse. I learned how my personality, moods, and attitudes were shaped by these relational traumas and challenges.

No one is likely to have internalized all the traits of codependency. In fact, in some ways, I found my childhood circumstances gave me an inner strength of character that was self-protective.

Because of my experiences with my grandmother and my husband, I wasn't easily bullied into submission. The downside to this self-protection was that I developed a high tolerance for belligerence and emotional abuse. The upside was an inner confidence that was unshakeable and ensured my willingness to seek and accept help.

Still, I discovered a level of shame in my emotional DNA that led me to live in a certain amount of denial and enabling as an adult. Although I did not let my family circumstances keep me from enjoying outward success, I built a hard shell around my heart and mind that I mistakenly thought shielded me from lifelong trauma and pain. I saw this protection as a personal coping skill.

I assumed I was in control of my destiny, from the standpoint of my educational, professional, and financial success, not realizing I surrendered my physical well-being and peace of mind to stresses beyond my control.

What I began to see in the mirror of my life was a wife, mother, daughter, and friend, who always felt stressed and besieged, who found peace of mind illusive, and always fought an uphill battle for personal control.

I was always fussing at something or someone, even while driving down the road alone in my car, but I never realized the root of this part of my personality until I gained new insights and self-discovery in recovery.

Just as the nervous system of the ones we love are highjacked by addiction, so are those of codependents.

I did not realize how long I lived merely in survival mode, mentally, physically, emotionally, even spiritually, until my mini breakdown. But that jolt of reality snapped me out of denial and forced me to admit my need to truly surrender to a power beyond my understanding for substantive help.

During my previous stab at Al-Anon, I realized I never fully surrendered to the idea of relinquishing control of my marital situation. I mouthed the words to the Serenity Prayer without fully understanding or embracing them: *God grant me the serenity to accept the things I cannot change. The courage to change the things I can. And the wisdom to know the difference.*

Until the shock and horror of my husband's alcohol-related seizures and my subsequent breakdown, I remained in denial about the dire consequences of his addiction on my life. My denial convinced me that only he was at risk.

The upside of my downward spiral was that my pain was the catalyst for new choices and an awakening to spiritual connection and guidance.

As I shared new revelations about myself in a new 12-step fellowship, I committed to stop reading my husband's inventory of perceived iniquities, to stop judging him, and to turn my focus on myself.

Instead of being desperate for him to change, I had the courage to see my own need for change, turning my attention instead to my own faults. I decided to stop trying to be perfect or controlling others. I let go of the belief that self-sacrifice and loyalty to a fault are signs of love.

To my greatest surprise, I learned that I lived a constricted life of unacknowledged shame about my family life. I limited my social life to family and friends who were aware of my husband's problems, and mostly to those who indulged his issues. I rarely invited others to my home or discussed my family with them. Growing up with an alcoholic maternal grandmother and father, I learned to hide my shame in the same way.

These boundaries I set were misplaced because I presented a false picture of my personal life built on secrecy and outward appearances.

The gift of 12-step sharing was the freedom to acknowledge the truth of who I was and what was really going on in my life, without shame or blame.

To support and be supported by others on the same road to personal empowerment.

To let go of my old story while writing a new chapter in my life.

To begin the healing that leads to freedom.

CHAPTER 13

The Love of Higher Power

When we enter a dark room and flip on the light, we see the illumination, without visualizing the electric power that is its source.

But if we place our finger in the socket through which the current flows, we experience a powerful shock, an invisible force that knocks us off our feet and makes our hair stand on end. In fact, electrocution can transport us from the realm of the material into the invisible world of the infinite.

That transference is how I describe my introduction to my Higher Power.

The shock of a nearly full-blown nervous breakdown that immobilized me that fateful morning and had me howling in despair, shot me into the realm of higher consciousness and a new life.

By admitting that my life had become unmanageable, I came to know and rely on God in a new and profound way. In a way far more personal than just believing what I was taught about God as a child.

I developed a personal relationship with my Higher Power that grew beyond merely praying to get my needs met. Through meditation and prayer, I came to understand and appreciate divine love and infinite intelligence as the grace and goodness of life. I found an inner wisdom that I could always trust and rely on, no matter the situation. I came to know this Higher Power more intimately as my God.

Every morning that I sit in silent meditation, prayer leads me further away from the pain of my family tragedies and into a garden of healing.

In the rooms of 12-step meetings, I was encouraged to "surrender" to a power greater than myself, without limitations placed on its name. This blind trust required a new imagining of Higher Power for me.

So, I decided to let go of the personified image of God as a white-bearded judge and ruler of the universe, because that likeness could not serve the needs of my circumstances. Instead, I opened my heart and mind to the Divine force that created the heavens and earth, something no earthly being could do.

What I needed was access to that higher guidance, intelligence, and wisdom. A comforting presence. A mystical understanding beyond my own.

I needed to be known, loved, and accepted, without judgment of my personal flaws and past mistakes. I needed to trust that my Higher Power also loved my addicted loved ones and was available to them just as to me.

As I placed my trust in a Higher Power, I recognized there was no quick fix for my problems, which is what I previously prayed for. I had insisted that God fix my broken husband and make everything okay.

Recognizing the pain caused by my codependent experience inspired me to make personal changes. I surrendered my will to a Higher Power who had an unspoken understanding of my needs and desires.

Rather than always asking for something when I found myself in a pickle, I opened up to a growing relationship beyond me. I sought to learn the lessons from my family relationships and to live in higher purpose.

Surrendering to my Higher Power meant embracing my freedom of choice. And my choice was to let go of disempowering beliefs that no longer served me, such as misplaced loyalty and self-sacrifice. I accepted accountability for my own life without trying to force my will on others.

At first, it's difficult to understand the concept of full surrender to a Higher Power when conventional social wisdom emphasizes power through control. Surrender is painted as giving up or throwing in the towel. When it comes to recovery, surrender requires you to give up all that you previously tried to control.

Surprisingly, I discovered my own power in letting go. Not all the answers, not needing to always be right, forgiving myself and others, and granting self-compassion for my personal missteps and mistakes. I found healing from frustration, blame, and resentment began as I surrendered my need to play the righteous victim to my Higher Power.

My conversations with God were no longer "foxhole prayers," that tried to strike bargains to get what I wanted. My spirit began to soar as I offered prayers of personal honesty, spiritual depth, and true substance. And each time, I experienced new self-knowledge and deeper inner awareness.

I released expectations of how circumstances should have been or could still be. Instead, I surrendered in gratitude to my life's challenges and tragedies as opportunities for spiritual growth. I surrendered in trust to omnipotent love and grace, and I affirmed in prayer my biggest dreams and deepest yearnings.

The more consistent I became in my spiritual practice, the more I was freed of past slights and pains. My heart opened up to greater love and compassion. When I stopped blaming my husband for my pain, I no longer felt like a victim. In the quiet of my morning meditations, my frustration and resentments melted away, replaced by supreme serenity.

I began to enjoy the experience of a budding relationship with my Higher Power as my life flourished. The stress of my situation began to melt away.

Over the last five years of my husband's life, his declining health forced him into what I perceived as semi-sobriety.

I described it as such because, as is typical of those who no longer drink but by no choice of their own, he substituted one addiction for another. Cigar smoking.

Addictive cravings, if left untreated, often simply transfer from one substance to another, because the brain remains in denial and the nervous system stays out of whack without some sort of sedation.

My husband's need to fill the void that alcohol once served with a smoking habit is known as "self-soothing" because it calms the craving. But this new habit was just as unhealthy as his drinking and actually quickened his untimely demise.

And so, a downward spiral of insulin-dependent diabetes caused vison loss, followed by renal failure and dialysis. As the years passed and required more and more medical treatment, his denial made him believe he could survive. But his doctors assured me he was living on borrowed time.

Sadly, he was not convinced, even when he lost the executive job that he loved so much because of the time he had to spend out of the office for dialysis and the limits that put on his ability to travel for business.

Unwilling to face the truth of his decline, he lashed out at me in frustration, even as my life blossomed. I never abandoned him because I had the growing support of my 12-step fellowship, new friendships, spiritual community, and prayer partners.

As I began to reclaim my life, I continued to educate myself on addiction and codependency, and got more deeply involved in the recovery community through Tommy Rosen's Recovery 2.0 and other programs.

I attended empowerment and motivational conferences, writing conventions, and retreats. I joined business groups and industry associations and became certified in empowerment and peer-recovery coaching. I also became a public speaker, accepting every opportunity to share what I've learned.

I am privileged to be mentored and guided by some of the world's most prominent spiritual leaders, including Deepak Chopra and the Rev. Michael Bernard Beckwith of Agape International.

Before long, new doors of opportunities opened that I previously only dreamed of, such as spending a month in Bali at Mastin Kipp's writers' retreat, where I wrote the first draft of this book. There I made some of the most special and enduring friendships of my life and maintain a strong bond of love with other women from around the world. We call ourselves the Bali Warrior Women Writers and support each other in all our endeavors and life milestones.

I've also since traveled to Egypt, South Africa, Cuba, India, and Dubai and had many other exciting worldwide adventures since losing my husband.

While it was heartbreaking to witness my beloved's tragic spiral toward the inevitable, fortunately, I developed a deep well of resources from which to draw strength. And I was comforted by his peaceful transition into the afterlife at home in his sleep.

My heart still aches, but I take comfort in knowing that the love of my life is now at peace and his demons no longer have power over him. I know the same for my dear grandmother and beloved father.

Since I surrendered any past grievances to my Higher Power, my life has been one of daily miracles. All because I chose the benefit of my own recovery.

I am forever grateful for the supportive resources made available over the years and I am committed to serving others in reclaiming the parts of their lives they've surrendered in self-sacrifice to a troubled loved one.

I share these experiences, not in rebuke of those I still love so dearly, but as a gift of forgiveness and redemption for their troubled souls and the earthly pain that drove them to the self-destructive path of addiction.

As one who has been redeemed by the gift of healing, I have come to know a new freedom. In these pages, I pray that you find the beautiful gift of freedom that is recovery from codependency, too.

Part 3

A Butterfly Rising

CHAPTER 14
A Butterfly Rising

The metamorphosis necessary for a caterpillar to emerge from its cocoon as a butterfly is painful and messy, but its transformation is beautiful. If the caterpillar resisted change, it would miss the opportunity to soar with the wings of a butterfly, in all its colorful magnificence.

Though recognizing the need for radical change is instinctive in the caterpillar, it is a matter of choice for those of us unwittingly stuck in dysfunctional relationships.

This is the stage where I meet my clients.

When they realize that they have no answers to the intractable problems of their loved one. When they realize they can't control the decisions and behaviors of anyone else, no matter how much they love them.

This need for radical change arrives when they realize that giving money, paying bills, making excuses, or tolerating disrespect and abuse is not a workable solution. Instead, they discover that their attempts to help are actually a deterrent to their loved one's choice for treatment for their substance-use disorder.

This place is where my clients realize they need help with changing their own enabling behaviors. By the time they come to me, they are out of answers, patience, and tolerance.

In the rooms of recovery, their unbearable frustration is referred to as "the gift of desperation." At last, they realize it's time for professional help and personal support to climb out of the mess of their relationship with someone who is out of control.

I call this the caterpillar stage of recovery.

For me, it was the point when I realized that my heart and mind were sick from feeding on a steady diet of addictive toxicity, neglect, and abuse.

And from my own experience, I'm available to those ready to wrap themselves in a cocoon of healing, personal recovery, and life transformation. In this place, my clients learn to detach from the problems of the ones we still love and allow them to be responsible for themselves while we focus on our own well-being.

Just like when the caterpillar outgrows its confinement in the chrysalis, acknowledging our own mistakes and unintended consequences is messy and uncomfortable, but crucial for miraculous change to occur.

I had reached this chrysalis stage when I experienced my mini-breakdown and diagnosis of traumatic stress. Because of a lifetime of trauma, I was ready for healing, so I wrapped myself in the cocoon of recovery.

After working to regain my bearings and overcoming limiting beliefs, I emerged as a butterfly rising. And so can you.

My role as a coach is to help my clients understand the limits of their efforts to fight someone else's addiction. I want them to recognize the difference between love and fear.

The power of addiction is beyond understanding. But it need not wield power in the lives of those on the sidelines of the addiction. Not if we come to terms with a few realities.

There's a difference between love and fear, but as codependents, we often are motivated by fear for our loved ones. So, we tend to enable in ways that actually support the addiction, such as giving money despite knowing it will be spent on drugs.

Although it may seem counterintuitive, we can't love that person from a place of fear. This worry makes us vulnerable to emotional abuse, manipulation, and control, all tactics they use to get us to support their substance use.

I once thought my relationship would improve if only my husband would get help. But when he checked himself out of rehab, I realized my hopes didn't match his determination to indulge his drinking habits. It was time for me to accept that he would win the test of wills. I decided that my life would only improve if I chose my own recovery, even if the circumstances of his life and health didn't get better.

I decided to become educated about the family disease of alcoholism and my inability to control others. Yes, my alcoholic family member was in a life-and-death struggle, but my fears served no purpose in saving him. My concerns only made him feel judged, ashamed, and resentful. And his reaction simply added to my own frustrations

This point is where my coaching program starts.

The sad truth is, we cannot save anyone who does not want to save themselves. But in educating ourselves about their struggles, we learn ways to be an encouragement rather than an obstacle to change.

By starting on our own path of recovery, we set an example and are ready to lend the support they need if they eventually choose to reclaim their lives.

Most importantly, we must each make choices that allow us to live our best life. There's no shame in seeking help for ourselves, especially when that's what we ask of our addicted loved ones to do.

I tell my clients all the time, "Never ask permission or forgiveness to do what's right for yourself and those you love."

Once addicts finally choose to get treatment, it's common for family and significant others to feel they have no part to play in the process of recovery. They mistakenly think that life will return to 'normal' once their spouse, child, parent, or partner returns home from rehab.

The truth is that the real work of recovery begins for the entire family once the loved one finishes rehab. Those who don't participate or educate themselves may become obstacles to long-term sobriety. Others may not understand that sobriety and long-term recovery are a lifelong journey with many challenges along the way.

It's not up to anyone but the recovering alcoholic or substance user to know what they need. Unsolicited offers and advice, such as, "You can have a glass of wine with dinner, can't you? After all it's not a drug," or "Why can't you go to the club with us? You're no fun anymore," may be detrimental to an addict's long-term success.

Teaching clients how to incorporate these types of tips and tools is my job.

Another crucial aspect of recovery is participation in a 12-step fellowship for families or counseling with a therapist who can help address years of shame, blame, and frustration. These outlets support true healing.

Most importantly, family recovery requires that everyone involved embrace change. Each individual must let go of old disappointments and resentments so old wounds can heal. It's necessary to let go of what coulda, shoulda, woulda been and accept what is.

As my clients surrender to the process of recovery, they make personal changes in their thoughts, attitudes, and behaviors that are beneficial to all areas of life.

My years of 12-step programs taught me many insights about myself I did not recognize before, especially how I was affected by and related to others. Over time, I learned to be responsive rather than reactive. I was no longer easily triggered or disturbed, which brought serenity and peace into my life.

I no longer focused on others as the source or solution to my problems. Instead, I learned to be accountable to myself. I stopped playing the victim or blaming others. I became more tolerant and mindful. Most importantly, I no longer felt the need to control people or circumstances.

These personal changes opened the door to a brighter future. And that brighter day is my goal for everyone I serve. The greatest benefits of recovery are self-love and freedom.

The addict and codependent get to reclaim their lost selves and stop the self-sabotaging behaviors that limit their freedom. The addict is no longer bound by their urges. And the codependent lets go of their compulsion to control others.

They both enjoy a new freedom.

Rehabilitation allows the substance user to confront the pain, fears, and trauma at the root of their addiction, while finding new joy and purpose.

I want my clients to be able to support their loved ones throughout this painful process. I teach them to leave the past behind and tap into an inner strength they didn't realize they had. They become open to talents and possibilities they were unaware of before.

Self-love grows from new friendships, new opportunities, and new confidence.

The codependent flies free of the dis-ease of co-addiction, leaving behind guilt, fear, and hopelessness.

Won't you fly with me?

A Butterfly Rising.

CHAPTER 15

Could You Be a Codependent?

This chapter contain questions that can help determine if my Certified Peer Recovery Coaching Program, Buttrfly Effect, is right for you. The following questions are intended as food for thought to start your practice of journaling.

Do you have addicted loved ones suffering from addiction: alcohol or drug abuse, gambling, eating disorder, or sex/love addiction? Who are they (be honest) (Check off boxes that apply)**:**

1. Parent
2. Child
3. Spouse
4. Aunt/uncle
5. Grandparent
6. Close friend
7. Lover
8. Other

How does their addiction affect your life?

1. Verbal and emotional abuse
2. Violence
3. Disrespect
4. Lying/cheating/stealing

5. Drunk or high daily
6. Household disruption
7. Constant arguments and fights
8. Financial challenges
9. Irresponsibility
10. Refusal to be accountable for their actions
11. Conducting illegal activities in your home
12. Bringing other addicts into your home
13. Chronically unemployed
14. Deteriorating health

How do you feel about the situation?

1. Shame and blame
2. Resentment
3. Embarrassment
4. Frustration
5. Helplessness
6. Confusion
7. Anger
8. Guilt
9. Disrespected
10. Abused
11. Shocked
12. Responsible
13. Put upon
14. Judgmental
15. Unloved

What have you tried to improve the situation?

1. Always letting them know they are loved and will never be abandoned
2. Making sure they have a home and all their needs met
3. Avoiding getting into arguments
4. Keeping tabs on them so they don't get hurt
5. Providing alcohol or drugs so they don't have to do anything illegal
6. Tolerating and excusing verbal and emotional abuse
7. Protecting them from the consequences of their actions
8. Searching the streets for them if they are missing
9. Believing their lies because you want to believe them
10. Saying 'yes' to things you know you shouldn't do for them
11. Accepting the blame for what is not your fault
12. Begging and pleading for them to go to rehab
13. Not insisting they be responsible in their affairs
14. Being loyal to a fault

Do you recognize what boundaries look like?

1. Not giving in to bullying behavior

2. Not allowing consumption of alcohol or drugs (by an addict) in your home
3. Refusing to argue with an intoxicated person
4. Calling authorities if violence is threatened
5. Not tolerating mistreatment or disrespect
6. Establishing consequences and sticking to them
7. Not allowing yourself to be put in harm's way
8. Having an exit plan in the event of any of the above situations

What keeps you from setting boundaries?

1. Fear of criticism
2. Fear of abandonment
3. Fear of rejection
4. Fear of punishment
5. Fear of upset and arguments
6. Fear of judgment

What patterns do you see in your relationship?

1. Repeated mistreatment and disrespect
2. Constant manipulation
3. Dishonesty
4. Being blamed
5. Boundaries always tested
6. Made to feel helpless
7. Constant chaos

8. Bullying
9. Disappointment
10. Selfishness

Is recovery for you?

1. I feel that if my loved one would get help for their addiction, the family dysfunction would end, and we could all be happy.
2. I am frustrated because my addicted loved one does not appreciate my love and loyalty.
3. I resent that my loved one doesn't seem to care about the fear, pain, chaos, and confusion they bring into our lives.
4. I walk on eggshells in order to keep the peace.
5. I blame my loved for robbing me of peace of mind.
6. I work hard to protect my loved one from doing fatal harm to themselves.
7. I seem to care more about whether they live or die than they do.
8. I fear being judged by others if I'm not supportive of my addicted loved one.
9. Being loyal and self-sacrificing makes me feel good about myself.
10. I fear being judged and criticized if I'm not accommodating.
11. I knowingly accept lies, abuse, and manipulation, excusing such behavior for fear of being rejected.

12. I will do anything to get my loved one to change, although I see no need for me to do the same.

What scares you about admitting your need to get help?

1. Not the one with the problem.
2. Judgment from others.
3. Implies you are less than perfect.
4. Seems like you bear some responsibility for your loved one's addiction and recovery.
5. Admission of failure.
6. Makes you seem weak and unable to control your situation.
7. The need to be strong for others.
8. Self-care seems selfish.
9. It's easier to find failure in others than to take personal inventory.
10. Hard to admit you might not have all the answers.

What scares you about personal change?

1. Taking a hard look in the mirror of your life and fearing what you might see.
2. Admitting you might not have it all together, and there's room for personal improvement.
3. Fear that others will not accept the "new you" and may criticize you for changing.

4. Fear of letting go of the familiar and comfortable.
5. Fear of failure when attempting a better life.
6. Fear of losing control.
7. Admitting you have more to learn about life.
8. Admitting fear and doubt.

These fears are the same reasons that addicts resist getting the help they need. **From an addict's viewpoint they:**

1. Resent the judgment of others.
2. Are unwilling to admit weakness and loss of control.
3. Resist wanting the approval of others.
4. Feel the shame of disappointing.
5. Dislike feeling vulnerable.
6. Suffer constant guilt.

These are just a few of the shared traits of co-addiction. The main difference is that addicts are helpless against the brain disease that keeps them in denial and their excuses are the way they remain in control of their lives.

Addiction is a selfish lover that draws everyone tied to it, whether directly or indirectly, into its destructive web. But as a codependent, you don't have to wait for the addict in your life to get help before you choose a better life for yourself.

What are the benefits of prioritizing self-love and personal care?

1. No longer reliant on others to feel good about yourself.
2. Not bothered by the opinions of others.
3. Being proud of who you are.
4. Valuing yourself apart from others.
5. Knowing you are deserving and worthy.
6. Being respected and treated well by others.
7. Being good to yourself.
8. Being true to your values.

What are the benefits of recovery from codependency?

1. A new sense of self-love and self-worth.
2. Freedom from shame and isolation.
3. A life of courage and dignity.
4. Putting to use painful lessons of the past to create a fulfilling future.
5. Healing emotional wounds.
6. Health and happiness in all aspects of life.
7. Healthy, happy, and supportive relationships.
8. Freedom from being controlled and manipulated by others.
9. Strong spiritual connection with a Higher Power.
10. Serenity and peace.

Recovery from codependency offers a chance to grow into new awareness and a joyful life. There's no need to feel like you are abandoning your troubled loved one. You simply come to understand that their life is not yours to control.

You have your own life to live, and there's no need to surrender your happiness and well-being to someone else's problem.

Once you take your focus off the problems of another and make yourself the priority, what might your life look like? You don't have to immediately have all the answers. There are no right or wrong answers since this is only about you.

What might you find on the road to self-discovery?

1. What are your personal passions, dreams, and desires?
2. What are your greatest achievements and talents that you can build on?
3. What would make you happiest and most fulfilled in life?
4. What have you learned from your painful past that might bring out the best in you?
5. How would you describe true success in your individual life?
6. What can you do now to begin building your dream life?
7. What qualities do you like most about yourself?

8. How can you put those qualities to work to serve others in similarly trying circumstances?

I'm Available to Help You. Follow this link to schedule a discovery call:

info@buttrflyeffect.com

Subscribe to my newsletter at: www.buttrflyeffect.com

And Subscribe to my Buttrfly Effect Podcast for advice from experts in addiction and family recovery, therapists, family members, and recovering substance users. Available on Apple/iTunes, Stitcher, and Spotify.

ABOUT THE AUTHOR

Gail Ferguson Jones is an award-winning journalist, podcaster, speaker, and Certified Peer Recovery Coach. She works with the loved ones of those who struggle with addictions by supporting them as they discover freedom from enabling and codependency. She was trained by the New Jersey Prevention Network in recovery coaching ethics. She was also trained and certified by the internationally recognized Connecticut Community for Addiction Recovery and did an apprenticeship with Tipping Point Recovery in Rhode Island.

Her **Buttrfly Effect Podcast** features conversations with experts in addiction and family recovery, psychology and therapy, as well as family members and recovering substance users.
Available on Apple/iTunes, Stitcher and Spotify.

Made in United States
North Haven, CT
18 November 2021

11246728R00090